UGLY DUCKLING PRESSE :: DOSSIER

God Was Right
Copyright © 2018, 2021 Diana Hamilton

Dossier Series

ISBN 978-1-946433-04-6
First Edition, Second Printing, 2021
Edition of 250 copies

Ugly Duckling Presse
The Old American Can Factory
232 Third Street, #E-303
Brooklyn, NY 11215
www.uglyducklingpresse.org

Distributed by SPD/Small Press Distribution (USA), Inpress Books (UK),
Raincoast Books via Coach House Books (Canada)

Design by goodutopian with the author
Cover image by Fernando Diaz
Set in Caslon with Avenir titles
Printed offset and bound by McNaughton & Gunn
Covers offset by Prestige Printing
Cover paper from Mohawk Fine Papers

The publication of this book is made possible in part by the National
Endowment for the Arts, by public funds from the New York City
Department of Cultural Affairs in partnership with the City Council,
and by the continued support of the New York State Council on the Arts.

GOD WAS RIGHT

DIANA
HAM

GOD   WAS

ILTON

RIGHT

CONTENTS

EXPOSITORY WRITING ON SOME KISSES

A woman wants to be kissed firmly and bristles at light pecks.

A woman wants to be kissed as if in an old movie: closed mouth, dipped.

A woman wants to be kissed only intermittently, as if she can't decide whether the kiss is a good idea.

She puts her hands on her breasts.

She pushes her against the wall.

She asks how she likes to be kissed.

"No, not like that. Imagine that I am a man, and kiss me again," one says.

"I don't want to imagine that you are a man. I would not kiss you, if you were a man, as you know," the other corrects.

"I'm sorry . . ."

"But I can lie and *tell* you that I'm imagining you're a man, if it pleases you."

"It does please me. Tell me how you would kiss me, if I were a man."

"I'd open my mouth wider, and I'd put your desire before mine."

"Do that, yes."

They do that.

She pulls back.

*

A woman wants to be kissed as if in the oldest movie: slapped in the face.

A woman wants to be kissed as if she's the old movie's unsung editor: given unmanageable reels of kisses good and bad to use to make one solid kiss.

A woman wants to be kissed by the woman dressed as the man in the old movie, but wants to know that's what's happening, unlike the woman dressed as the woman in the movie.

*

"Would you really not kiss me, if I were a man?"

"You know I'd kiss you no matter what."

"How have other women wanted to be kissed?" she asks.

"It depends.

"It's true that the women who mostly kiss men, when they kiss a woman, sometimes kiss bigger and with less patience, but then that's also not true, sometimes the women who kiss mostly women kiss entirely impatiently, you've just entered the house and kissed their cheek and they're already on their knees."

"I like to be kissed that way."

*

Here's an old story:

You're kissing me against this wall & saying shit

like "here are the reasons I'm not going to kiss you" but

I can't hear you, my ears are only open

to the sound of your gasp, you say

"The final reason I'm not going to kiss you is that

I don't kiss those I've already kissed, I'm only

interested in new kisses." You repeat

this. Your hand moves up my skirt, you're

a woman, a woman who says "it's too bad

I'm straight given how much I love kissing you"

or "It's too bad you're straight

given how much you love kissing me

and how you just told me you're not straight

a moment ago, I love you, this is the real

reason I'm not going to kiss you, I love you and

you don't love me you told me so you said

'I have a lot of love for all of my friends'

I'm not an idiot I have some pride I can't

kiss you, I'm a man, I have a woman, she isn't

you she doesn't love me the way you love me

but there are promises a man makes."

*

One says: "A woman told me she liked to be kissed wetly, like where the strings of spit connect your mouths when you pull away."

The other responds: "I kissed a woman who likes to be kissed one kiss at a time; she needs to mark the end of each kiss."

"You have to be patient to kiss that way."

They describe more kisses, and they try each of them out.

This, of course, makes them fall in love.

The game takes years, and remains very fun.

One day, though, one realizes she hates to be kissed just after dinner. The other realizes she only wants to kiss right after dinner, they have a fight, it ends in kisses, one realizes she hates to kiss and make up, they have another fight, they kiss again.

This starts an awful, circular fight, one that gets in the way of their research.

They eat, one kisses, they fight over the timing, they make up, they kiss, they fight over the timing, they kiss, they repeat until bed.

Now they just have this one kiss: the make up kiss, which one of them hates.

But they're glad to be stuck in this loop, secretly.

It puts off one kiss they don't feel ready to try.

A woman wants to be kissed goodbye, for example.

PERSUASIVE ESSAY FOR SEX ED

"Here are some strategies," the teacher says,
"for consent, and for how to balance it

with what will surely be your growing sense
that 'eagerness,' of a certain type, can be a turn off."

She passes out a list. She leaves room
for discussion, lets them generate

at least two new strategies of their own,
each: "Pretend to not be into it

in a way that, like, makes it clear you're *really* into it
but know better than to act like it,"

one says. "Tell everyone at school you want her
but then act bored when she's around."

*

"At some point," she advises, "You will find yourself
underneath someone

you wanted to have sex with before
they got on top of you, even though

it now feels like you'll die
if they don't get off of you.

Your first instinct might be to get them off
as quickly as possible, which you'll presume

requires you to feign pleasure in case
they're noticing this upcoming death

of yours, the years you'll spend near vomiting
at the memory of how you did this, daily,

for a year, so you moan, you find the fastest
route to their orgasm, you put your feet on the nearest

wall to provide resistance for more apparently eager
gyrations, they take forever to come, it becomes clearer

that you hate it, they finally roll off and ask
'Did you come?' and you say 'In my own way.'

This is a bad first instinct.
Find others."

*

"Ideally, you shouldn't sleep with anyone
you have to persuade to do so."

The student writes this, among other things, down.
She thinks about the earlier texts:

"Come over"
"Ohhh, you know I want to do, but

I have a ton of homework"
"You can do it tomorrow,

I won't keep you up *too* late"
"I'm still not sure where things stand with Emily . . ."

"Let's not invite Emily, then."
"omw"

*

No one talks, she thinks, anyone else into sex
in Jane Austen's *Persuasion*,

even though the whole book, as far as she can tell,
is about love, and being talked into or out of it.

Anne is persuaded not to marry, though, so—she thinks—
I guess she is talked *out* of sex.

And Anne's so often the object of a sentence's
action: "The absolute necessity of

seeming like herself produced then
an immediate struggle."

Though it's very important not to confuse active syntax
with consent: It's not just "He raped her" or

"He was raped," It's also: "He was struck
by the ease with which she gave in" or "They quit resisting."

The student writes many such examples, divides them
into two columns, looks for recurring

structures, forgets to pay attention
to the teacher, who, she gleans

from the snippets that break through, is talking
about ways to eat out a menstruating woman.

Anne: "If I was wrong in yielding to persuasion
once, remember that it was to persuasion exerted

on the side of safety, not of risk."
The student copies this down, from memory,

at the top of a clean sheet in her notebook.
For the first part of *Persuasion*,

persuadability is an error: Anne wouldn't be
unmarriageable, still longing, had she not given in. Then,

persuadability is safety: Louisa ignores
advice, and cracks her skull.

Her English class agreed
it was a mistake to find

a thesis statement on whether it was good
to be persuaded, in this book, or out of it:

it is more a question of decisions
made in context, and of Anne's

becoming a strong adviser herself,
one to whom she can turn.

*

"Here are some other instincts
you might have: 'I just need

a minute, can we just lie here
a second and maybe take it slow, I'm sure

I just need to regain my senses.' Your partner,
if they are not a rapist, will understand, but

this might not work for you either: the minutes
you take will feel like hours for both of you,

you might know you'll talk yourself into it
and by that point the having-hesitated

could make your attempts at physical reassurance
all the more dramatic. Or you might just lie there,

hoping they will not want to fuck a corpse,
but even though they don't want to fuck a corpse

they want to fuck you and they might try to be understanding,
'Maybe this is just the way she likes to have sex,' they might

tell themselves, or 'Maybe I can give her instructions
on how to have sex a better way,' they might tell you.

Or 'No, that's not the way I like it,' you might try,
hoping to provide directions that make

the whole thing less miserable, but
everything they try will be a bit off.

Instead, try: 'I've changed my mind, I'm sorry,
you're so beautiful, I'm just not into it, can we

go for a walk, I understand
if this makes you want to leave.' Don't suggest a movie,

you'll be tempted to as you wouldn't have to
leave bed or speak during a movie,

but they might assume you've changed
your mind and try to get on

top of you again. Don't suggest drinks,
as whiskey may get rid of your anxiety and/or disgust

and make you want to sleep with them, after which
you will never know whether you were too drunk

to have really changed your mind, you will hate them."

*

The student takes careful notes. She is in love
with a man who is an alcoholic and

with a woman who is her best friend
and with another friend who is not attracted to her

and with another friend who is attracted to her but not to her gender
and with the teacher, who often rearranges her hair

and who seems like she would probably be good at sex.
When the man is not there, she wants him,

when he is inside her, she wishes she had insisted
on a condom, when she is on top of him, she wishes he knew

where her clit was, when she is sleeping with the best friend,
she doesn't remember he exists, when she is drunk,

she kisses everyone, some of them seem to regret it,
she apologizes, when she is sad, she looks for love

and instead finds sex, when she is happy, she looks for sex
but finds love, she does not believe this, she is not sure

she has ever had an orgasm, she is afraid to find out
she has been faking it the whole year, with everyone,

even with herself, when she is with herself, she never thinks
of a man on top of her, when a man is on top of her,

she thinks of a woman beneath her, when a woman
is beneath her she thinks of a woman on top of her, etc.

*

"You will not die," the teacher continues,
"from 'regrettable' sex. But regret and rape are different.

And even certain kinds of regret
will mess up later sex that you otherwise might have liked,

and you want to look out for that future self, to give her
the chance to enjoy being pushed against the wall

of the shower without having to map that wall onto
other walls she was pushed against."

*

"This is how you prepare your asshole for anal.
This is how to tell a partner you really want them

but have a yeast infection. This is how, if you are a man,
you can tell a woman what you like in bed

without sounding like a misogynist, even if
what you like is legible as a performance of misogyny,

this is how you ask someone how they like to be kissed,
this is how you deal with realizing someone hates the way you kiss,

this is how you proposition someone and accept rejection,
this is how you proposition someone and accept them changing their mind."

*

The student's phone buzzes, she takes it out
and sees a text from the man asking her to come

over after school, she goes, he's drunk, naked, hard,
she smiles, smokes a joint, climbs into bed, winds up beneath

him, realizes how bad her yeast infection is, hides the pain,
moves slowly to reduce friction, he asks her to move faster,

she moves faster, her whole vagina feels like it's on fire,
she rolls onto her stomach so he can't see her cry,

he hears her cry, he pushes her away, "What the fuck,"
he says, "You said you wanted it, don't

put this shit on me," she keeps
crying, she tries to explain.

ESSAY ON BAD WRITING

I.

This is a bad poem
by a lady poet.

It's called "Essay on Bad Writing,"
but I want to talk about writing that's good.

Initially, this was a bad essay
called "Bad Poems by Lady Poets,"

after George Eliot, who wrote "Silly Novels by Lady Novelists" as if she were
a man, but she wasn't:

> Silly novels by lady novelists are a genus with many species, determined
> by the particular quality of silliness that predominates in them—the
> frothy, the prosy, the pious, or the pedantic. But it is a mixture of all
> these—a composite order of feminine fatuity—that produces the larg-
> est class of such novels, which we shall distinguish as the *mind-and-mil-
> linery* species.

I'll make a claim
grounded on an impression, rather than on history,
here: that Eliot's criticism relies on a reasonable, yet false,

> —hope that women will be taken seriously as writers if they write about
> more serious things,

> —assumption that they're writing themselves into irrelevance by lim-
> iting themselves to what subjects and syntaxes and heroines they think
> the world already permits them, and

—belief that to be "not silly," they have to write like writers who have been taken Seriously, to show that to write well is not Manly, but something any writer can do.

To the contrary:

—women are taken more seriously as writers right now, I think, if they start from what seems "silly" and "feminine"—fashion, sex, confession, gossip—and insist on the seriousness of this silliness;

—and then present as "silly" more "serious" feminine woes, like rape or abortion;

—and then show that none of this is silly, that representations of women—even "silly," rich women, rendered comical by the tragedy of their lack of purpose—are serious representations.

—and it's good that women have various strategies for writing, of course.

2.

I've been uncomfortable, lately.

I bet you have been too.

It feels like, lately, to be a "lady poet," you have to act a little silly: you pretend to be dumber than you are, to fake upspeak and self-doubt, to refer to Serious Theorists while flipping your hair, all

"I swear I didn't read this Adorno too closely; I promise I was too busy starving myself."

I get it:

It's sexist that High Rising Intonation (HRI) is associated with stupidity.

It's anti-intellectual to presume self-doubt means one hasn't thought hard enough;

> —everyone who's ever been smart at all—just like anyone who has ever really had faith, in God or in Love—is completely plagued by doubt.

But still.

I'm not sure the men watching know this,
and I like to watch women
be masters of discourse.

Unfortunately, part of that phrase troubled you, if you read it carefully, and has troubled me:

3.

I like to watch women.

Whether they're mastering their discourse or not, honestly.

But mastery isn't an escape from the question of sexiness; it pairs really well, in fact, with tousled hair.

The question of "whether" to be sexy, or to bring up the question of your own sexiness, while being a writer, is an impossible one:

—it's a really fucking difficultly specific gender performance to get on stage, as a woman, and give the impression you don't give a fuck whether you look good.

I would love to give this impression, personally.

I definitely don't: it's obvious that my poems, like many poets', and despite my best efforts, are accidentally in the service of a larger desire to be desirable.

Silly poems, by a silly lady poet, i.e., me.

Unlike Eliot, though, I know better: you can eschew this silliness, and write really well, about more "universal" things like Men or Money or Going to Work—things men believe books ought to be about—and no one will read your work.

If they do read your work—because they are your friend, or because they actively struggle against sexism, or both—

they'll be sure to find out it's about Women. They won't let women's writing touch them.

They may even have gone to too much grad school to remember that books can touch them, that writing is inextricably tied to subjectivity, and to the body, no matter how many times a computer writes a poem.

And unlike Eliot, I don't think there's anything actually Silly about the super-serious violence of gender expectations.

I'm getting off-topic, and I'm getting sad.

And OK: the title here is "bad," not "silly."

But I want to stick with silliness a bit:

with the performance of comfort with being positioned as interested in appearance, in luxury, with no pretense to a "neutral" performance under capitalism.

Because men and women aren't so different, you know. It's a false construct, I hear.

Men are silly too.

4.

Recently, there have been at least three men taking luxury baths in their poems.

What does this mean?

When I started writing this, I wanted to make a joke:

That when a straight man takes a luxurious bath in his poem, it's a signifier for a more interesting relationship to gender.

That when a woman, straight or gay, takes a luxurious bath in her poem, it's a suicide note.

5.

Perhaps the problem wasn't that ladies were writing the "*mind and millinery species*" of novels, but that not enough male novelists were admitting that their heroes spent time picking out hats.

Or taking baths
in lavender and salt,
or with iced coffees in their hands,
or as part of an elaborate morning toilette.

As in D.A. Miller's description of Jane Austen's
mockery of Robert Ferrar's "will to style"
in *Sense and Sensibility*,
where Robert's ridiculous dandy-ness, while he tries
to pick out a toothpick case, "reveals the Woman in him."

But Miller sees a darker move at work
in Austen's mockery:

this Woman's "blatant presence fails to rid him of the smallest bit of male entitlement."

I think this is related to what Trisha Low was saying
when she reviewed Brandon Brown's and Steven Zultanski's recent books.

She says that both have written books that

> "interrupt our conception of the subject to make eloquent critiques of their gendered positions as straight white men."

This is at the review's end, where Low compares the feminine and masculine "confessional" and what they can *do*. But she disagrees with herself,
or at least, loses faith in their eloquence: they failed
to sufficiently harm themselves in the process to truly fuck with that position.

Whatever critique of masculinity they both offer,
I think she's saying,
they can't use the form of the confession
the way women can—as a kind of a performative risking of the self—
"until men are accused of actually possessing essential character flaws because of the kinds of work they are making."

I don't agree with Low here, entirely

> —perhaps because I have fewer stakes in the question of confession, and because I do think that men are accused of possessing essential character flaws because of the kinds of work they are making (although her longer comments about the risk of harm are different in kind). And because I don't think the history of confession as a laying-bare of the self can be uncomplicatedly tied to femininity—perhaps these male poets are just putting themselves in a line from Augustine to Montaigne to Rousseau.

One thing Low suggests that I keep coming back to, though:

That these poems fail to give up the position of male privilege because they're too good.

They're too well written to seem seriously engaged in risking the self.

This is a great argument to me:
that men need to try to write worse.

This is one way I got to the question of "bad writing."

6.

Here's another way I got to that question:

A few years ago, I started writing another essay as a joke. The essay asked: do women have the *right* to write bad poetry?

But I'm leaving out a backstory I want to provide, without making this essay about that context.

Last year, an editor of an online magazine wrote to me requesting a specifically negative review of a specific poem:

> "dear diana," it began, announcing its informality early on, and continued, a bit further down:

> "we're wondering if you'd like to write a negative review of patricia lockwood's "rape joke"? i still sit up straighter when i think of 'triggers.'"

The email contained little else, other than the identifying information.

What is the issue, though?

When I first received this email, I found it
confusing, but relatively innocuous;
to the extent that I was offended, it was for my own sake:

> the implication was that the (male) editors of the magazine wanted to
> criticize Lockwood's much-circulated and much-loved poem, but felt
> that they needed a woman to do it. Even better, a woman could write
> it who had also written a poem about rape ("triggers," referred to in the
> email) and previously published it in their journal.

To be honest, I was not nearly as bothered by this request then as I am now.
My refusal was friendly—I thanked them for thinking of me.

I came to see it differently when the same editors published a ranting (sexist,
ageist, the other adjectives you'd expect to complete this list) critique of a
number of contemporary poets in their final issue, for which the negative
review was solicited.

I rehash the existence of this bullshit
essay only to talk about one common response I heard

> —all, I should say, from writers who regretted saying so once we had
> more time to think about the issue—

7.

"Sure, it's fucked up, but what's *really* offensive is how badly written it is."

I remember saying a version of this myself: I had found the writing so annoy-
ing that I had stopped reading too early to even find out it was offensive.

Only later that night, drunkenly arguing with a friend, did I hear my own
retort:

"How could a lack of stylistic clarity be "more offensive" than rape jokes?"

(Yes—the editors wanted a negative review of "Rape Joke" to run alongside their own rape threat.)

I frequently hear writers observe the priority of "bad writing" over other offences, though.

It seems like one way of redirecting attention,
however sloppily, to the issue of writing
itself, I imagine,
and it comes from the recognition that lots of art
has justified its offensiveness
by way of some other merit.

But if "bad writing" is a description that can cover up the offensiveness of someone else's writing, it is more often used to cover up one's own shittiness:

　　—In the comments section to "The Rape Joke," as well as to Lock-
　　wood's follow-up post, you can read all kinds of people pretending to be
　　more worried about quality poetry than about rape.

By which I mean that their pretense to concern
seems like a thinly-veiled way of voicing their anger that someone made them think about her rape.

These circumstances share the hope of replacing
a more difficult explanation of offense
with the idea of good or bad writing.

In the context of this poem, it means finding
another, more "intellectual" way

　　to tell a woman she should not have spoken, which women are often
　　told, but especially when they

1. Intend to tell a story that implicates men's role in the horrifying normalcy of sexual violence, on which much has been written recently, or

2. Put themselves in the position of Speaker, of Writer, of an authority not first given to them by someone else.

I wrote this part last year, during a context of another moment of everyone-on-my-internet talking about rape, when I was binge-reading stories of assault, crying, and hating myself for the fact that it meant I wasn't getting my work done. I quit writing this for a while.

Then, I came back to this essay a few months later, in a week full of accounts of assault in what is known as the alt lit community.

(This same week, my high school ex wrote to me to ask if I was following the alt lit stories, and to ask a favor: *I've been secretly afraid that you and maybe one of my other early partners would write something about the shit I put you through when we were young. If you were gonna do that would you talk to me about it?*)

And again, what's *really offensive*,
according to people all over the internet,
    is how bad the sentences are in these men's novels.

And these are the people on the right side, the side that believes the accusers!

They're equally happy to have an aesthetic they hate connected to assault as they are supportive of the victims.

(You don't even want to read the shitheads on the "other side,"
    the side that uses phrases like "grey area" and "witch hunt" and "ruining a young man's life with a Serious accusation;"
the people on the wrong side are seriously concerned that these accusations might hurt the writing scene:
    "Perhaps the end of HTMLGiant spells the end of the sentence.")

While the latter is far worse—at least the first only hopes to find evidence of shittiness in the prose quality, rather than excusing shittiness for prose quality's sake—they are both stupid.

8.

So I'm writing this essay after all, to say:

Fuck you if you think bad writing is more offensive than rape.

9.

And so—what about bad poems? Should we care about them, when there are more important things to care about?

Of course, I think we can care about all the aesthetic descriptions that add up to an individual justification of a "good poem" *while* caring about whether the poem is violent, and while caring about the fact that the place to fight certain violence is largely outside of poems, as it requires a more violent strategy than poetry normally offers.

But let's return to Low's point: that bad poems might be good.

—That men need to write worse poems if they want to take on the position of femininity.

(She doesn't say that, but that's how I'm reading the end of her essay.)

—That we need silly poems by male poets, that is, as a larger struggle towards changing women's relationship to silliness, or badness, in poetry.

And that the move from "bad" to "good" happens in small ways; the "badness" of feminine content providing a way to think through a poem's critical relationship to constructions of gender.

But also:

that we can't determine, in advance, what aesthetic will produce a "good poem,"

that we can't determine, in advance, what "content" or "form" will be adequate to a better idea of "good,"

and that we can think through the relevant questions—like,
    is this a good poem?
    how does this writer perform/address gender?
    what is the relationship between this poem and bigotry?
    what formal strategies is the writer using?
    if this poem hurts people, are they people I want to hurt, too?
    have these formal strategies historically been complicit with things the
    writer doesn't want to be complicit with?
    if so, is it fair to say these strategies might function differently in the
    context of this specific text than in others?
    why is s/he/they writing about this subject?—
    in relationship to each other.

10.

So the men can start writing worse poems
    —and not "worse" as a replacement for "offensive;"
    don't forget, we're going to quit worrying about "bad writing"
    when people are writing sexist garbage

    —and not "bad writing" in the sense of
    "needs to be workshopped by jerks"

    —but "worse" in the sense of "less serious."

and I'll be happy for them, and I'll read them.

But "then" "after" "men" "start" "writing" "bad" "poems"

(that are "bad," in this case, in a "good" way, i.e. they somehow resemble "women's writing.")

11.

Someone has to write "good" "ones."

"Good ones," that is, that engage
the recurrent and often painful need to exaggerate
or reject outright or caricature or ignore
or sexualize or otherwise modify
the poem's performance of gender,
without recourse to a dumb "natural" way-of-being
from which this exaggeration could be said to emerge.

12.

Serious Poems By:

ATTEMPT TO BE ADEQUATE TO THE EXPERIENCE OF LOVING AN ANIMAL

So, given the question, "did dogs have a Renaissance?" the answer is clearly no; dogs did not partake of the intellectual debates which define the period, nor did they have the concept of historical periodization.

—Nigel Rothfels, *Representing Animals*

When I saw the small goat attempt to walk, but stumble, then find
his footing, leaning his head against another goat,
then turn his head back over his shoulder to look at me, then nuzzle
an udder, then let his ears fall over his face, as if playing shy,

I wanted to be able to write.

I wanted to write a poem, even,

about the way people who love animals,
including and perhaps especially me,
including and perhaps especially goats, feel

when they didn't know they were going to see animals,
but, suddenly, they do.

It feels, I tried to dictate into my phone, the way I imagine it feels
when you, at once, believe in God and believe that She has blessed you.

But this is not sufficient.

The internet does a better job of documenting
the way we feel when something soft, especially
a mammal, is very cute, than poetry does.

Not just the internet:

    —children do this better than poetry does

        (factoring in that children and poets are overlapping sets);

    —children's poetry, for example, knows that it should be about animals
    more often than adults' poetry does,

    —and maybe photographs do it better as well, although they can get a
    little too serious

        (the experience of seeing a goat doesn't have much to do with
        framing, although lighting can make their fur pop);

    —they document, at the very least, the fact that you were so moved by
    the animal that you wanted to share with someone else the way you
    felt when you saw it;

    —non-human animals also do this better, as they respond to the appeals
    of other animals by smelling, fighting, pawing, kissing, hunting, sing-
    ing, jumping, or otherwise letting response itself take priority over
    their ability to share this response with someone else, convincingly;

    —even fiction documents animals better than poetry does, in that ani-
    mals more often get to represent animals, rather than standing in for
    non-animal experiences or feelings,

        (even if, while serving as a narrative dog, the dog has a non-dog
        allegorical function).

It's not true that I didn't know I was going to see the goat, though.

I had walked down to the fence to see this specific kid, in fact,
but instead, I found two big donkeys

there; when I had walked down yesterday the donkeys weren't
there; they must have been hiding from the rain.

So I was in fact heartbroken by the surprise of the donkeys.

They were not the baby goat, though
they moved to reveal the goat

I had come looking for, which made me smile, and when I sat down to try to write, inside, I lied, I said I didn't know I would see a goat, because I had decided that, according to the poem, the feeling I had for the goat was predicated on not expecting to see one before it came into view, because that was the feeling I had had last night, the point at which I didn't know I would see one,

rather, the point when I first saw the goat—surprise came earlier.

I felt surprise when I read that the place I was headed had "farm animals,"
and I hoped that among them were baby goats,
but I thought January would be an inappropriate time
for a goat to be a baby.

If you were wondering, January turns out to be a very likely time for baby
       goats:
I have seen at least six.

I would have seen eight, but two of them were lost to the winter.

I insisted on feeding the mother who had lost two kids
extra carrots, because I interpreted her lesser willingness to fight
for baby carrots evidence she was mourning,
although I do not know.

The unneeded milk hanging heavy from her udders is a certain kind of
       mourning.

A poem to capture the feeling of reading a pdf
that informs you there's a chance you will soon see
the absence of a baby goat in a field where its mother
might or might not be aware of its absence.

I texted someone to ask them if they had any fave books/
movies that were love letters to animals.

Either this could help me write the poem, I thought, or it could lead some-
one to try to impress me,

a feeling akin to love in the way
reading about an animal is akin.

They said *Au hasard Balthazar,* a movie
I have texted them about a lot, which gave the impression they were avoid-
    ing the question

    —and, I thought, it should be obvious to them I was thinking of this
        movie, since I was staring at two big donkeys when I texted,
    —who, by the way, have very big mouths, lips so big you must get your
        fingers between them to make sure the baby carrots don't fall out, even
        though this risks getting your fingers between the teeth, which seem
        very strong,
    —although they might not be strong, as another pdf informs me that
        "dental disease is second only to hoof problems as the most common
        medical condition of the donkey"
    —"donkeys have a finite amount of tooth available"
        and it is hard, after having seen this movie, to look at the hide of a
        donkey
    —without seeing it as if through the lenses of love, torture, and/or Bres-
        son's camera.

I was annoyed, but unfairly: I hadn't texted them a picture of the donkeys,
but of the goats.

[interlude in which a series of memes representing the cuteness of goats signals that this is about the use of memes in the poem and not about the goats themselves.]

[interlude in which I show Shiv a video of goats calmly balancing on a teeter totter and he insists they are CGI, revealing that neither of us can distinguish a real goat from a fake.]

[interlude in which an analysis of the material costs of Au hasard Balthazar's *production attempts to measure what resources might be needed to write a love letter to the goats.]*

I expected to see cows, but they are further away in the distance than the donkeys, goats, and horses.

Closer to me are the photos of cows in Lydia Davis' *The Cows*, which is among the most mysterious stories I have read.

—I believe it to be a religious text, in the sense that I believe calming down when looking at the face of an animal is religious.

Reading Rancière is not religious. But he says

—Bresson looks at the donkey in *Au hasard Balthazar* in the same way that
—Flaubert looks at shit in *Madame Bovary* (he says something more complicated than this, I know, but he also says this), and
—*Madame Bovary* was best translated into English by Lydia Davis, author of the mysterious *The Cows*, so perhaps she draws on some way of
—Flaubert's looking, to look at the cows as
—Bresson looked at a donkey, but I think
—her style draws on her translations of Flaubert's correspondence more than of his fiction; she does not write like Flaubert, except perhaps in terms of a shared attention to diction; so
—she would look at the cows the way Flaubert looks
—at the blank page: Davis reads F.'s letters "to know him better and to hear him grumble, usually, about *Madame Bovary* and the experience of writing it"
—I also ask this of the cow in front of me, as I have by now walked over.

I am scared of him. It is very stupid that

I am scared of him. I realize now that he is

a bull, because I text

"look at this cow" to someone, who responds,
"with horns!"

I was walking home the weekend before Christmas in a little bit of a sad state.

I had just purchased a very ugly single pearl earring as a Christmas present for a man who had said he wanted a pearl stud;

> —knowing that he would in fact be unhappy to receive a Christmas present from me, I could not buy him an expensive one, so when I found a $5 earring, I thought,
> —"this will do, I can honestly present this as not a gift, it's too shitty to be a gift, but it also shows that I remember a wish he once expressed, which is a sign of love, I'd like to give that and not a Christmas present,
> —'I will buy this earring.'"
> —They didn't let me buy just one. I thought "maybe I'll wear the other one, like we are 10 year old bffs,"
> —but the earring was honestly too shitty for me to wear.
> —He was holding my cat, whose evil is proportionate to his perfection, days later, when I said, "oh, I found this cheap earring & remembered you said you wanted a big pearl. It's obviously fake but it might look great on you."
> —He said it was too big and refused to try it on.
> —The earring remained on the bedside table until he left in the morning, when I moved it to where I keep my other unappealing jewelry.

I ran into a friend who is a poet, on this walk.

She asked me why I was walking

that neighborhood, and rather than explain
the earring or the man, I explained that I had just finished

reading a very good book at the coffee shop,
Cervantes' novella *The Dialogue of the Dogs.*

I offered her the book:
> —you should read it, I said, two dogs discuss philosophy, and the human
> narrator who frames the story where the dogs talk tries to "prove" to
> his interlocutor that the dogs talked, that he isn't lying, because, he
> says, the dogs speak so much more intelligently than he can—he must
> just be reporting overheard speech.
> —The dogs proceed to show all that is horrible about the organization
> of human society.

The poet responded by referring to the people in graduate school who do
animal studies, how she likes many of the texts but never quite understood
it as a discipline.

We talked about how it's weird to read

The Animal That Therefore I Am with graduate students, because they read it

as if it is an authoritative text on the human/animal divide,
rather than a cute first-person account of one philosopher
who is strangely embarrassed by his cat seeing him naked.

(I am a very embarrassed person who hates her body and talks to her cat, and
my only concern when I am naked with him is the fear he will claw off my
nipples.)

When you say that you are writing a poem that will attempt to be adequate
to your feeling of loving animals,
and when you run in a certain academic circle,
many people mention *The Animal That Therefore I Am.*
If I had not left my hometown it is less likely

that anyone would tell me to read *TATTIA*,
though it is likely I would still be making this attempt.

    —Brian tells me that his cat refuses to look at his dick and that
    —cats are very different from each other and some of them won't look
    at you when you're naked at all;
    —"Derrida's wrong," he ends.

"Once, at a graduate school party," I told the poet,
    —this was a Halloween party in which I was dressed as a leopard, fwiw,
    —I was telling a man about my dream of opening an animal sanctuary
    that would also be an artists' residency/living space for people other
    than cis men to hang out with cats, write, and otherwise recover from
    the various traumas of their lives before and after the sanctuary.
    —The man, a scholar of animal studies, pressed me on whether I would
    allow tomcats at the sanctuary, given the gender restrictions on human
    residents.

I said yes.
    leading to a very long, drunk argument in which I confessed my belief
    in the functionality of the human/animal divide.

I told this story to the poet on the street at great length, the earrings in my
bag, while distracted by thoughts about what a bad omen this already-failed
giving was of my certain coming heartbreak—I was not thinking at all about
the story I was telling.

I presented, nonetheless, large examples of my argument for a functional, if
not real, difference between "humans" and "animals," alongside my apologies
for the examples' problems.

For a moment I was pleased
    —that neither of us were graduate students anymore and that
    —both of us were standing on the street talking about whether animals

exist, and
—coming to the agreeable conclusion that they do.

I pressed the book into her hand.
She put it inside her bag of falafel.

Some believe that refusing to eat animals expresses love.

Others pray, lovingly, to or in thanks of the animals they eat.

Still others refuse to prioritize the lives of animals
who die for meat over the lives of the humans
who die for richer people's vegetables,
meats, fashions, medicine, devices, manicures, etc.

Some in this latter group make an effort
to modify their behavior to minimize harm
to animals of all kinds, without making an effort
to modify the broader world.

Some in this latter group make an effort
to dispel the myth that individual consumer choice
is an effective way to modify the world even
when it feels like the only kind of choice
this especially shit world affords us.

Others work on the world itself: not to modify it, but to destroy it.

Some stop there. Others, to build a new one.

Still others throw up their hands.

Many, across these and other subgroups, carry on: a difficult to determine
number of them have watched, 1,224,593 times, a looping clip of an otter

"dancing" between a rock and a branch in an artificial environment designed to imitate nature, with a slightly longer clip of Outkast's "Hey Ya" playing over the loop.

Initially, the otter has a single paw on the rock ledge in its enclosure, the other paw reaching up to a tilted branch.

As the dance begins, it repositions
its hands ("Hands that can grasp, eyes
that can dilate, hair that can rise
if it must") to control its movement: first,
putting its weight on its left paw (the "branch"
arm), then putting both paws on
the branch, then moving to put both paws back
on the rock, all the while gyrating
in a way that resembles human humping.

24 people, a relatively homogenous set, at least considering their shared habit of engaging actively with content on the *Washington Post*'s website, comment on an article about Khanzir, the only pig living in Afghanistan, after his mate and children were murdered by a bear at their shared zoo.

The comments range from Islamophobic "jokes,"
to those praising the zoo for caring for an "innocent creature of God,"
to those taking the opportunity to argue on atheism's behalf against all religions,
to those noting that pictures of Khanzir indicate that he's in great pain because no one is trimming his toes,
to those admitting as counterevidence the lives of wild Afghani boars.
The jokes rely, unsurprisingly, on either the animalization of people or the personification of animals.

Animalization, according to Neel Ahuja, "involves contextual comparisons between animals (as laborers, food, 'pests,' or 'wildlife') and the bodies or behaviors of racialized subjects (Ritvo 121-27; Pratt 208-13)."

Ahuja furnishes examples:
"W.E.B. Du Bois denounces post-Reconstruction industrial schools
—that failed to treat African Americans as "more than meat" (94),
leaving them in a "terium quid" between human beings and cattle
(89).
Ngũgĩ wa Thiong'o recounts that punishment in British schools for
speaking Gĩkũyũ included wearing a sign
—declaring, "I AM A DONKEY" ("Language" 437).
Frantz Fanon describes the rejection of animalization as a basis of
national consciousness among colonized peoples
—(who ironically declare their humanity with a "roar") [...]"

The article focuses on the last example: putting on
an ironic "animal mask."

Fanon: "For they know that they are not animals. And at the very
moment when they discover their humanity, they begin to sharpen their
weapons to secure its victory."

Subjects who escape racialization get to wear
a different animal mask: that of the empath.

In understanding and feeling for animals' perspective, for example,
Patricia Highsmith's stories of animal revenge
might seem like an argument for rejection of animal cruelty
as a path to rejecting human cruelty.

Perhaps she preferred women to animals, though:
she describes how a "frosty blonde" in a mink coat, one
who made her feel "swimmy in the head, near to fainting"
as "she slapped her gloves," inspired *The Price of Salt*.

Todd Haynes makes the relationship between fur and lesbian
desire stronger—Carol's coat is a main character, albeit one
with an unreliable actor: pieced together from scraps
of vintage coats to produce the color that costume designer Sandy Powell
wanted, "the coat itself fell apart every single day," forcing
an assistant to spend "her entire lunch time repairing it."

Highsmith had the kind of life think pieces love to summarize:

> "She was a smoker and an alcoholic, a bisexual who never stayed in a
> long-term relationship, and supposedly, a cruel misanthrope who pre-
> ferred animals to people."

So far so good.

But the more responsible sources will throw in a line or two—
in between rhapsodic accounts of her many lovers—
acknowledging that she "could be prickly, racist
and overtly cruel" or that "she hated Jews, women, taxes,
literary agents and her mother's nursing-home bills," etc.

Typically, Highsmith's racism appears near a paragraph on the snails
she carried in her purse, as if a mere eccentricity, or near the one
on trying analysis to cure her of homosexuality, as if
the product of unrelated suffering, or near the decline
in her writing's reception, as if the product of personal failure.
Most acknowledge that she hated indiscriminately (and most evidence
of her anti-Semitism focuses on supporting the Intifada)
and all avoid the conclusion that, at least in terms of her feelings
re: animals and humans, Patricia Highsmith looks like a PETA model in
    trousers.

Love of animals is dangerous.
The same feeling that makes it True and Right

also makes it a point of shared understanding with "bad" people,
    —people who happen to like animals and are bad
    —which happens often, let's admit it.

The fascists and the communists and the college friends and the friends
    from home alike all share cat memes.

I was asked to have lunch with a donor
to the nature preserve where the baby goat lives.

We ate Panera salads. He had been visiting this house, built in 1844,
since he was young. He would sleep in a hammock
that is no longer here, but "the marks of which can still be seen in the old tree."

No other talk, at this lunch, of scars, or trees, in this house in Kentucky
    from 1844.

I am good at this.

I love listening almost as much as I love talking, which is to say, a lot,
    —it is easy for me to admire someone who can carry on a conversation,
    —who can narrate their life to a stranger simply because food has been
      put between them.

I looked for a point of overlap.

We found one in animals.

    "I'd rather photograph birds than shoot them, now
    . . . if my old hunting buddies could see me
    filling up the bird feeders each morning."

He described many dogs, a parrot
who has been with him for 25 years, able to imitate

both his voice and his wife's, a college snake, a crow,
some squirrel friends, a baby raccoon: it was an impressive list.
He choked up describing the recent death
of a baby goat under a wooden structure
they had added for the goats to play on.

He was eager to tell me that
many members of his family were vegan.

Love of animals led to other loves:

How happy he is now that he does not work,
how blessed he feels to be able to share his wealth,
to support artists, to volunteer to assist a local photographer, to pay forward
the generosity he received as a young man
that he knows made his life possible,
to understand what *matters*—as animals do.

And yet.

We talked then of schools: those we went to, how we felt about them.

In the middle of trying to express
something else, he complained
that the schools in Louisville were "ruined by busing."

We argued, unclearly, briefly.

He "corrected" himself.

Then, he gave me a print of a photograph of an eagle
        —taken by an artist he's financially supported.
        —This man and I grew up
        —just a few hours from each other, and

—had much in common.

—The eagles, goats, and cats permitted us

—to stay "in common."

"Each new day," Davis' *The Cows* begins

"when they come out from the far side of the barn, it is like the next act,
or the start of an entirely new play.

They amble out from the far side of the barn with their rhythmic, grace-
ful walk, and it is an occasion, like the start of a parade."

When I say that Davis' cows are mysterious
to me, and that, in another sense, the book feels religious,

I am trying to talk about a combination of faith and doubt in her description.

"It is like the next act;" every day of the cows' walking turns life into a very
long play.

Maybe a new play has to start because they don't come out altogether the
way she expects:

"Sometimes the second and third come out in stately procession after
the first has stopped and stands still, staring."

This is different play. The first cow
seems to have become a protagonist. There is one cow
who can be distinguished from "the cows," which is the first step
in a love letter, someone becoming specific
who was once part of a generic group.

"They come from behind the barn as though something is going to
happen, and then nothing happens."

Now I am no longer trying
to find out how sure she is
that this is "like" a play, nor am I worried
about how many acts it has.

I want to watch the play.

I certainly feel as though something is going to happen,
even though she has told me it will not.

"Or we pull back the curtain in the morning and they are already there,
in the early sunlight."

And now I learn that the play I have been looking forward to
—watching the cows come out, as they do each day, or at least twice,
"from the far side of the barn,"
—might not happen every day after all.

For a moment, I'm anxious.

I know that I've left behind the goat
to whom I would like to express my love.

But then I reread Davis describing how the cows move:

"They are motionless until they move again, one foot and then another."

It is easy to have a lot of confidence in this description.

This is pretty true of cows.

I think that, to write a love letter
to the animal, perhaps you should try to describe it
accurately. You still have to compare it to things,
because comparison is a part of love, but the more literal
the comparison, the more loving.

I am going to call the speaker "Davis"—as a "metaphor."

Davis also finds these cows mysterious.

They move without her seeing them move. She is

> "surprised that the cows are so often visible, because the portion of the hedge over which I see them is only about three feet long, and even more puzzling, if I hold my arm straight out in front me, the field of my vision in which they are grazing is only the length of half of a finger."

There are at least three fragments in this one quote
that I have unconsciously plagiarized
in my own writing. This surprises me, as
    —this is the first time I am rereading *The Cows* in many years,
    —I am heartened, it suggests I am carrying this book around with me, and if it has the mysterious properties I believe it to have, I have been protected,
    —I have had recourse to the calmness of this description of cows as a way of thinking about or describing other things,
    —not only animals, also my non-animal feelings, if I have them,
    —my anger at my own body
    —last night I dreamt that, after having been accidentally hired to model in some capacity with many beautiful and/or small women, I looked in the mirror to discover that in the process of gaining lots of weight, new giant red bands of stretch marks had formed across my back,
    —but it was too late to be upset, because I had already accepted the description of myself as beautiful before being presented with this contradictory evidence.
    —My dream remembered that I had read *The Cows*, and when it saw the fatness of my body in the mirror, it stepped back from interpreting it:
"Yet she is getting bigger, so she must be coming this way," I said to my own body.
    —On the other hand, when men describe my body objectively, it is not calming.

—One, when I was 18, had never seen large stretchmarks before, I guess. He asked,

—"Where did you get these tiger stripes?"

—I was not relaxed by the comparison to cats.

—Another, more recently, asked, "What are these bruises all over your legs?"

—"They are not bruises."

—"What are they?"

—"They are just there, I can't do anything about them."

—"Are they the start of varicose veins?"

—"Yes," I said, collapsing onto the bed in the lingerie I had hoped he'd find persuasive for a change in activity, but instead burying my face in the blanket,

—"I don't know how I didn't notice them before," he offered,

—"Me either," I muttered, extremely sad, because I imagined in three years he had registered and accepted these veins as, at best, having no negative effect on his desire,

—and now, in my failure to change the activity, I had only evidence the noticing had offered a counterargument to the expensive, latticed, high-waisted underwear I was wearing, the pattern of which he proceeded to trace—"It's almost a pentagram," he said,

—I fell completely apart in the face of what followed, more noticing of my body without desire as response to noticing,

—we can do this to animals. But you can only "objectively" describe the body of a lover if you also intend to register desire, in your voice or movements, sometime soon.

For ten years, I have been trying to write a poem
that would be adequate to the love of animals.

At first, I wanted to write a poem that would be adequate to the way I felt
when I looked at the picture of the mouse with a human ear grafted onto
      its back;

I thought the uselessness of this ear,
which is just a burdensome, flightless wing,
said something Important about people and/or listening.

But it was not a poem about the mouse.

    —The mouse was asked to go to work to teach us about a non-mouse
      purpose, which is not like a love letter at all.
    —"Darling, I can't stop thinking of you, and it's really helping me with
      the concept of codependence in this article I'm drafting," we don't
      write to each other.
    —Nor should we to animals.

Even before that, 15 years ago, I tried to write a poem

about the death of my dog, Jenny, but it was instead a poem

whose true ambition was to demonstrate how mature I was

(though it ended with a scene where Jenny and I pee on the bathroom floor
      together);

Before that, 24 years ago, I tried to write a poem

about the murder of some baby robins by a local blue jay.

    —I was trying to relate the concept of "being a predator"

—to the experience of "being a blue jay"
—to determine whether a blue jay could be faulted
   for this murder.

My mom was helpful.

—She explained that animals could not conceive of sin, aren't responsible
—for being good the way people are, because our badness is the effect
—not of our actions, but of our knowledge of the idea of "bad."
—I came to the conclusion that, though I understood,
—I still hated blue jays, and always would.

Otherwise, though, her guidance helped: I forgave animals.

But when my kitten died young, soon after, I would not forgive God.

—He should, I insisted, have taken me, a sinner.
—I lay prone on the floor, 10 years old, demanding the kitten's life be
   returned in exchange for mine,
—who knew, after all, enough about "badness" to pass judgment.

"Animals are 'inarticulate.'"

This line is more specific:

"They do not leave documents,"

Nigel Rothfels laments—

would-be animal historians
have no primary texts by animals,
he says, to analyze.

Of course, we believe some animals are articulate.

I, an animal, am trying to tell you my feelings,
although I could make an "inarticulate" attempt to do so.

When we are sad, we are often inarticulate.

Koko the gorilla can give some account of herself.

For example, she uses counterfactuals to tell jokes.

This is just the kind of "lie" Kenneth Koch recommends
in teaching poetry to children.

It works, especially if kids find out themselves:

I asked some 4th graders to write a line like
        "I wish I was a _____ but I'm really a _____"

and they started literally:
        I wish I was rich but I'm really a poor student.

Quickly, they learned they could wish wilder:
    I wish I was a lion but I'm really a boy

before the class "troublemaker" tried inversion:
    I wish I was a boy but I'm really a giraffe

liberating the class from any more sense-making.

To make a counterfactual into a joke,
the theory goes, you have to know enough
about what the other expects to fuck with them:
Koko must be able to predict how others feel.
This skill (making poems about wanting to be animals,
making jokes, as an animal, about wanting to be understood
by human animals) reflects a growing "theory of mind."

More than her irony, though, Koko is known for her pets:
she asked for a cat for Christmas in 1983,
and the dick humans tried to pass off a "lifelike stuffed animal"
as the real thing, not with the generosity of a lie
designed to make a friend laugh, but the condescension of a lie
you think you'll get away with.

She did not play with it and continued to sign "sad."

For her next birthday, the humans gave in—

she got to choose a kitten, a male

Manx whom she named "All Ball."

Unlike his stuffed replica, All Ball escaped

and was hit by a car. All Ball died.

They told Koko, and she understood.

She tried to explain how she felt, signing,

"Bad, sad, bad," and "Frown, cry, frown, sad."

Patterson also reported later hearing Koko

making a sound similar to human weeping.

MEMO ON TWO POSSIBLE CONDITIONS FOR OUR MARRIAGE

TO: X

We cannot, of course, get married—but if we did, there are two ways.

1.

It would be most fun to marry you when it's a terrible idea,
because it's too soon, or
because it's being posed as a solution to our problems, or just
because you know the relationship won't work out and this seems like a way
of putting that off, of being people who surrender entirely to a mutual whim.

That's why, right now, I sometimes want to marry you.

Especially in my dreams,
where as long as we've been together,
you have proposed and I have refused:
"Why are you ruining this?" I ask.

2.

It is of course more reasonable to get married when it would be a "good idea,"
which is like walking to the bank one afternoon to take out cash to pay your
rent, but finding the whole experience relatively appealing despite its con-
text—either the sun is especially nice and your bank is in a neighborhood
in the city you like to walk through, or it is raining, and you would never
have gone for a walk in the rain if you didn't have your rent to pick up, but
suddenly remember how much you like it, how convenient an umbrella is,
etc. The specifics aren't important: what matters is that this totally routine &
actually bad experience appears as a pleasantly specific Tuesday lunch break,
somehow, and you walk home and hand $800, taken out in twenties, to the
landlord, and you smile.

i.e., it sucks.

1A.

To get married when it's a bad idea,
but a romantic solution, is like
waking up that same day, realizing you cannot afford your rent, but knowing
you need to do something, and going downstairs and seducing your landlord.
You don't begin by saying you can't pay your rent—you half want to believe
you're just there to fuck him, after all, by coincidence, of your own desire—
but you make some excuse to go inside (you're thirsty, you want to say hi to
his small dog) and wind up between him and a wall, as if the kiss were yours
to surrender to. He doesn't mention the rent, of course, and you go back to
your apartment and fall in love, you wonder if you can sustain an affair with
the landlord indefinitely, or whether you'll need to somehow get the kind of
income that makes a non-stressful walk to the bank before the affair goes
south, or the landlord gets the courage to mention the rent to you, or his
wife finds out.

Most of all I would like to marry you like a tenant who fucks her landlord
     for rent,
pretending she does so out of love.

2A.

I refuse to consider marrying you
years from now, when "all is settled," and neither of us has yet been killed
by errant taxis on our individual walks.

It isn't "imaginable."

To do neither, to not even date, or make up, or quit
hurting one another needlessly,
to agree to just kiss and talk about Bolaño all day, is fine.

It's charming, even,
in the way not paying one's rent at all would be:
in a much more pleasant walk, comprising fantasies of the bank's explosion,
or with no thought to money at all, which passes through too many hands, as
I will myself, once out of yours.

FIVE-PARAGRAPH ESSAY ON THIRD HEARTBREAK

¶ 1.
"Above all," the narrator of Elena Ferrante's *Days of Abandonment* instructs
herself, "don't give in to distracted or malicious or angry monologues.
Eliminate the exclamation points. He's gone, you're still here."

She gives in to monologues, of course, she exclaims, she doesn't
even remain "here," in the real apartment, lives instead
in the apartment that splits open, rots, breaks, like she does:

"You'll no longer enjoy the gleam of his eyes, of his words, but so?
Organize your defenses . . . don't let yourself break like an ornament,"
it goes on, citing de Beauvoir's *The Woman Destroyed,*

citing Ferrante's own recurring poverella, citing her own monologues,
the ones to which she gives in. By reading *Days of Abandonment*
alongside the saddest fucking songs, like Dusty Springfield's

"You Don't Have to Say You Love Me," Sinéad O'Connor's
"Nothing Compares 2 U," and Lee Hazelwood and Nancy Sinatra's
"You've Lost That Loving Feeling," and by rereading

a failed poem one woman wrote immediately after being
"destroyed," lol, we can see that the woman is normal
and, for that reason, entering a depression, evidenced

by the following three examples: 1. fantasies of doing well,
2. fantasies of doing badly, and 3. fantasies of reconciling
the first two, such that, just like Ferrante's

Olga, the self-directed instructions to regain control function
mostly to provide narrative evidence that she is,
so to speak, out of "it," as they say, out of a story.

¶ 2.
"I'm doing much better than I expected to be," she said,
with some regularity, for the first few months, "I've been spending
a lot of time with friends and a lot of money, ha, but

I don't feel like I'm dying." She'd emphasize the last word,
making it clear, to some listeners, that by bringing up "dying"
she was entertaining it. Alone later, she'd try to write a poem:

"Once, I thought / it would be important to change—/
a new breast, scar, style, symptom, pain, fire, lay, death, body,
would make it bearable." She referred here to an earlier poem

she wrote after the second breakup, where "Starting
with the right nipple," she would disfigure herself, become
religious, ugly, transform into various creatures. "Eaten up, then,"

she wrote in this new poem, "I'd listen to 'You Don't Have to Say
You Love Me,' on repeat," when she still believed
"some reduced presence / would be better than absence . . .

Not this time." In the new poem, instead, she imagined staying
the same, waiting two-three weeks for her skin
cells to fully regrow, applying nail polish as a measure

of when she'd have nails that hadn't clawed him. She counted
the number of years (two) before her hair, with regular cuts,
would replace itself. "In this way, remaining just the same

produces our best evidence of chronology's terror."
That sounds sad, but it was meant to be "positive," about how,
"When your heart is broken, women want to know if you'll survive.

By doing so, you prove, perhaps, that they too will survive."
In order to survive, she put off reading *Days of Abandonment*,
for which everyone agreed she was not ready and gave up

on the poem because, though it was meant to be about staying
just the same, she kept rewriting the same line:
"Still, it's sad not to die of a broken heart."

¶ 3.
Since trying to be healthy was a sign of depression, she figured
she'd try, instead, trying to do badly. "Proving to women,
by surviving, that they will too, assumes the women identify

with you. Assume instead they compete with you; show them
this won't happen to them, that they won't have to survive
because no one will leave them, because they, unlike you, are lovable

still, they aren't the sort of people who get constantly drunk, kiss
everyone, make their friends uncomfortable, fuck the cab driver
on the way home, somehow remember the fucking, stay in bed

sad for the next three days, weakly type emails of regret, etc.
Show them you had this coming," she instructs herself, "Fall apart:
'Of all means of dying,' you wrote yesterday, 'the refusal

to simply give oneself food and water is the most appealing.'" We see how
she's trying to stave off the Hazelwood for the sake of the Springfield,
i.e., not to have lost the loving feeling, but to maintain it at all costs.

This about-face, "I'll go running every day I'll be beautiful
I'll realize I have better conversations with all of my friends" to
"I'll refuse to do anything until someone hospitalizes me for sadness,"

it's even more damning than the second impulse on its own.
And pathetic, too, because all the fictional representations of "destroyed,
comma, a woman" at least rely on daily life with children.

She doesn't have that excuse, has only her fragile sense
that she had been writing a story with confidence for some years
only to find herself unable to win out against an editor

who wrote in an ending so stupid, so unrelated to what came
before, the whole story became dumb but somehow
also more "marketable." She had no kids. She had a cat,

and for this reason the death of Otto in *Days of Abandonment*
was much worse, she saw herself whipping the cat,
hating it for loving him, burying face in fur, it bleeding to death.

¶ 4.
As the girl read of Olga's apartment growing solid again, the cellist
handsome, the friends less afraid to look her in the eye, the girl wondered
if this division between "doing well" and "doing badly" was false.

"No: If I could give myself permission to see him worth dying
for, which I don't, my favorite way to go would be to hold my breath,"
she wrote. The "which I don't" perfectly represents the third sign

things were bad: the desire to maintain both the desire to die
for him and the knowledge he is worthless our surest sign yet
she was fucked. She went for a run

but listened to "Nothing Compares 2 U" on repeat,
she ate alone and decided it did, contrary to expectations,
take away these blues, she went home and

wrote new lines to the bad poem, now rational
rather than hysterical, she read it aloud to her friends
who were all very high, she announced, they were

having a great time, "the best time," and admitting this,
she said sagely, did not mean she hadn't been devastated; it meant only
that she knew how to take care of herself, and how to ask for help,

she added, a very important skill, one Olga has even in her worst
moments, with the ghost of the poverella and the daughter's assignment
to stab her whenever she seemed to be fading away, she knew to ask

the daughter to stab her the man who had failed to fuck her
the night before to save her the phone to work please her brain
to quit betraying her, to remember the son sweating in the room,

like Olga, she told her friends, I may lose my mind but I know
where to look for it, she put her legs in the air and held her
belly and laughed, can I read this Ferrante quote to you, she

asked without waiting for a response: "'Because I was forced
to do that torturous work of analysis for Mario,' see," she explained,
"women have to become scientists of love when

men are just dumb parents who refuse to tell you
why they believe in God, they say some things aren't for analyzing,
I have to remain evidence the love was real while really

working to find out what went wrong; I have to draw charts
of my panic attacks, map them onto my childhood and his,
map them onto the body of the new woman, I have to

get to the point where I can say, as Olga does, 'I don't love you
anymore because, to justify yourself, you said that you had fallen
into a void, an absence of sense, and it wasn't true …

'No. Now I know what an absence of sense is and what happens
if you manage to get back to the surface from it,'" she read, she said
"I want to say this and mean it, but to do so I have to fall

into the void he pretended to, in order to understand." Her friends
put on the song by the man about how he's sad his ex-girlfriend's having fun
dancing and getting laid and making new friends and dressing sexy.

¶ 5.
From the girl's experience, from Ferrante, and from songs, we learn
that you do not get rid of exclamation points by deleting them; they slip
into the small intestine, come out as diarrhea, they slide up the vagina

and rub against the part of the clit you can hit from the inside, they
make a girl sleep around; her feelings hide the exclamation marks
in her pasta and they get caught in her monologue.

Of course, she did not accept being trapped. One day, she heard a story
about a man having to leave a woman because she gave him, for their first
anniversary, a knife, an omen he couldn't live with. He left her.

She, our girl, not his, went back in time, as if in a story or in a movie
where the genre does not change but accepts nonetheless the signs
of other genres; she visited their first anniversary; she gave him the knife.

She knew it would take a while—four years—for him to know
to leave, because he is so slow at analyzing love's evidence. But
she was patient, she waited, and when it happened, later, it made sense.

EPISTOLARY ROMANCE ON LOVE AND FRIENDSHIP

Dear Shiv,

You told me to write to you.
It was kind of you to tell me to write.

You were writing to me
of heartbreaks and hangovers
and whether we'll ever love or write again,
and how to replace one
with the other, with each other.

You were asking me how to tell the difference
between love and friendship; no, I was writing
about that, not you; no, not yet, I hadn't started writing,
that's why you told me to, so I started writing
to you, and since you are love & friend
I thought about the difference between you & you, you
who appear in my poems as Shiv and in yours as Shiva
and in countless boys' poems, I'm sure, as a man to kiss,
just as you do here, just as you do in Jane Austen's
Love and Freindship [*sic*] where you knock at the door.

In this book, you're a suitor to the woman
Deceived in Freindship and Betrayed in Love;
look at how we can spell love
but we can't spell friendship,
that's what Austen tells us
about having been young.
Let me spell it out for you:
You knock at Laura's door,
and everyone notices:

My Father started—"What noise is that," (said he.)

"It sounds like a loud rapping at the door"—(replied my Mother.)

"It does indeed." (cried I.)

"I am of your opinion; (said my Father) it certainly does appear to
      proceed from some uncommon violence exerted against our
      unoffending door."

"Yes (exclaimed I) I cannot help thinking it must be somebody who
      knocks for admittance."

"That is another point (replied he;) We must not pretend to deter-
      mine on what motive the person may knock—tho' that someone
      DOES rap at the door, I am partly convinced."

Here, a second tremendous rap interrupted my Father in his speech,
      and somewhat alarmed my Mother and me.

You hide behind the names Lindsay
and Edward, you fuck Laura because your dad
told you to fuck Dorothea, "Never shall it be
said that I obliged my father," you tell her.
She hears you, she knows you oblige not
your father by fucking her but your mother.
No, you oblige neither: you die in a carriage
where you travel in secret with your wife's
best friend's husband; the best friends
lament their loss. This is a lie, too:
You were not Edward but Sophia,
I, Laura, we're best Freinds, which means
we listen to each other and disregard
our parents and constantly faint, scream, and
go mad, which is what we are doing today.

That's why I'm writing to you. If I didn't
we would both be fainting into a glass,
pretending to mourn our husbands, but actually
on a trip together where we give no fucks about anything

but each other, this my understanding of our roles in
Jane Austen's juvenilia, let's move on.

"No," you tell me, you're not ready to move on, "tell me
more about this epistolary novel Jane wrote at fourteen,"
you demand. I don't have to, Shiv. You never tell me
the plots of what you watch and read; it makes me mad.
I come home with a lover, and I'm happy to put off sex
to wait for you to tell me the plot of *Duke of Burgundy*,
which you just watched, you tell us, and which, you tell me,
has no men in it at all and is instead about the dom/sub
relationship between the two women. "Where is the Duke?"
I want to ask, but instead I say, "tell me about it"
and you say, "no, I don't want to give it away, I want you
to watch it." I am furious about this, and the lover
takes your side, so I'm furious at him, too.

You wouldn't tell me about *Duke of Burgundy* so
why should I tell you more about *Love
and Freindship*. Clearly, the movies' women are *friends*, but
all you'll tell me is that there's a role reversal, so I give you
my copy of Jean Genet's *The Maids*, which I've been texting
excerpts of to the man as an attempt to flirt
but should have sent to you, everything to you, except
what you ask me for, because it isn't fair. First,
you have to make it up to me, which you do,
not by doing anything, but by being replaced:
just as we can replace lovers with porn, we can replace friends
with plot summaries of the films they've watched.

Now, look here, Shiv, I'm disappointed; I assumed this movie
was old. You know I thought it would relate to the 1937
Désiré, which we watched together recently, about a valet
who has seduced the mistress of every house he serves,

and about the sex dreams they have about each other, but
now I'm accidentally reading about a movie from 2014;
this is disgustingly recent; I can only *imagine* how short
each shot will be. OK, it's getting better now. I see that
it involves lovers writing each other scripts! No one
will do that for me; I'm furious again. You knew
all that, but you wouldn't tell me. The maid,
Evelyn, is fucking her boss, Cynthia, who abuses
and punishes her for her failure, but "things
aren't as they seem," aha; it is the maid who instructs
the mistress to abuse her: "While Evelyn finds the scenes
to be sexually exciting, Cynthia only acts them out to sate her lover."

This is also what happens in one of Serge André's
case studies, "Dany, ou le choix du masochism."
Dany knows what he wants, which is, we'll both agree,
quite a lot for one man to achieve, but he can't get it:
every woman he finds to beat him does it
out of kindness rather than desire: "in order for
that scene to satisfy him, an essential condition,
although rarely fulfilled, was that his partner really
derive pleasure from whipping and humiliating him."
He gets married; his wife complies; Dan
Savage never tells you what to do about a wife
who's *game* but who doesn't enjoy the game herself;
poor Cynthia, *pauvre* Dany; we all spite our lovers'
generosity. Our friends' refusal to sleep with us
is so much more generous, as they don't do us
the violence of putting a real person's needs
in the place of their roles in our fantasies.

Instead, you ask to wear my dress; I say "yes,
of course, anything;" you put it on; I say
"you look great." I look great too. I'm in your button-

down with tights; we kiss a little but not too much.
For the remaining years of our lives what follows
this kiss is both of our guesses; it doesn't have to
happen; we don't have to lose the sense that,
say, were I to top you, I'd do so from my own
desire; I'd tell you to shut up, "Shut up, Shiv,"
I'll never say, "This is for me, not you."

Thank you. Thank you, Wikipedia, for standing in
for Shiv to tell me the plot of the movies he watches
so that I can tell him the plot of the books I read
without the need to punish him for withholding.
It is not Laura who writes letters to Marianne, but
Austen who writes for the pleasure of her family:
"Arm yourself my amiable young Freind with all
the philosophy you are Mistress of; summon up all
the fortitude you possess, for alas! in the perusal
of the following pages your sensibility will be
most severely tried." Shiv, I've tried
your patience. Try mine, now. Tell me the plot,
not of the movie you watched most recently—
I've gotten over this anger; I thought only men
refuse to tell you what happens in movies, until
my friend scolded me for telling the bartender why
Jeanne Dielman is great; "just see it," she cut me off,
making it clear the problem was not that others refuse
to summarize what they've seen and read, but that I refuse
to see anything someone I love hasn't persuaded me
is worth seeing; I lack the trust necessary to believe
anyone who says "just see it;" "try harder," I want to say,
"I know you can tell me the detail that will make me
watch. If you saw *Ninotchka*, for example, you would say
'there's this line where Ninotchka says, "We don't
have men like you in this country," and the dude thinks

it's a compliment; he says "thank you," but she says,
"That's why I believe in the future of my country;" but
that's not all, she falls in love initially not with a man
like him, but with a hat, which she sees in a window
display and pretends to despise: "How can such
a civilization survive which permits their women
to put things like that on their heads?
It won't be long now comrades.'" If you'd
said this to me, I would have believed
you; I'd have sent myself an email saying "WATCH
NINOTCHKA, THERE'S A HAT," and maybe
I'd forget to watch *Ninotchka* for a long time,
but when I did, I'd see the hat and I'd think,
"Shiv was so generous to tell me of this hat,
so that I could anticipate seeing it later." But,
as we know, *blessed are those who believe
without seeing*, i.e. blessed are those who watch
the movies their friends tell them to watch
without demanding they spoil them—tell me
instead of the plot of your love life.

"You know that story already, Diana," I know
you'd say, "it's about love and friendship;
it's about figuring out whether Love is so big
it doesn't matter who is a man or a friend
or a woman or hetero- homo- or otherwise
mono-sexual in a direction that precludes
neither friendship nor love, but sex, but the sex
and its absence or occasional near-presence
or presence in various forms is enough
of a problem to call into question both
love and friendship, neither of which ought
to require sex, if love is this big, the sex
should be big too, not little, you know

about sex with friends." This is not about me
and you, note, but about our other friends,
the ones with whom we actually had sex
instead of just talking about it all the time.
It's not just me who knows something
about that; it's also 18-year-old me, who wrote
an essay titled "Sex with Friends"
for her freshman comp class.

I was even more of a snob when I was little.
I quote Aristotle, Heraclitus, Berger, and Gray
to prove that women, like ancient Greek men,
need not eschew sex to avoid
objectification, should instead fuck each other
to enjoy the full friendship I believed men had
in Ancient Greece; later in college, I would read
Montaigne on friendship, his sadness
that women aren't worth talking to and men,
we "now" know, in 16th century France,
aren't allowed to have sex with other, so there's
no relationship good enough: just
sex with boring women and love with men
who won't let you kiss their neck. But
there's a way out, I argued: to recognize that
sex isn't that important, and then have a lot of it:
"In recognition of the comparable triviality
of carnal desires to friendship, people can learn
to balance both," I wrote, when I was 18, when
I had already fallen in love with at least five friends
who weren't attracted to women at all, let alone
to me. I wrote letters home to my then boyfriend
listing all of the straight women I had fallen for;
I described Annie's eyes and hair all I could
to him; I was sad about it, sad that I still wanted

something other than him; I told him so;
I still thought that if I read enough books
(if I had the sex with books Montaigne recommends)
I'd find a way "out"—out of the closet I'd left
a long time ago, but found myself back in
each time I held a man's hand in public;
out of Indiana, which I had left; out of men's
hands entirely and into the hands of friends.

When I found this old essay, I assumed
it would argue for sex between women;
I didn't remember that, at 18, I was worried
about men: in the essay, I'm angry
one of the readings strongly implies that
women's "activities" are more fulfilling
than men's: "Gray limits men and women equally,"
I say. I bring in a "personal anecdote"—the teacher
had required us to write a "personal essay"
that included "a story from our real lives,"
but I thought I was too good for women's
writing, i.e., too good for a writing of the self
(I was wrong), so I instead wrote a pretentious
philosophical argument for my own daily
longing—and I recounted men in the dorm
I overheard talking about paying a woman
for sex not because they wanted to sleep
with her, but because "we want to demonstrate
the power we hold over her." This story doesn't lead me
to argue that 18-year-old cis men are worthless
pieces of shit you should avoid by fantasizing
about your best friends; it leads me to argue
that people of all genders learn to build friendships
that make room for desire. I still had hope.

Last night, Shiv, you said,
"We should actually just get married."

It's what we both want: for friendship to prove itself
so prioritized with respect to other loves that it takes
the form of those other loves; further, we want love
to be so "important" it doesn't matter than I'm a woman
and you aren't attracted to women; I want to love
a man without holding his heterosexuality
against him; we both presume "friendship" precludes
shit like "jealousy" and "children" and "arguments
about dishes." We're wrong, though.

Our friends were right
when then said we should never marry.
God was right when he made us
want to marry each other, but showed us,
with a series of heartaches we'd have
only each other to process,
there's no way to make truth
out of the lie of partnership—
I won't be Jane Bowles to your Paul,
not only because I'll never write that well,
but because we only imagine
they were happy; we don't know;
perhaps one lay awake crying
while the other got head in Tangier.

2ND ESSAY ON BAD WRITING

Once, I wrote
that poetry doesn't make arguments: it does

something else instead, I argued,
in an essay that was not a poem.

If I had argued it in an essay
that was a poem, it might have been

"interesting," where interesting just means
"there's something to be said about that,"

and what I might say about that would include
some acknowledgment of the intentional contradiction

meant to complicate a clearly reductive idea
of the work poetry can or cannot do with something "clever."

But I wasn't being clever, when I wrote that.
I was being naive, so

I was wrong, when I wrote that, and I'm probably wrong
still, I was defensive, when I wrote that,

I was defending "poetry," I thought,
but Poetry doesn't need my defense.

It can make its own arguments.

I was defending "aesthetics," I thought, but I was wrong
when I wrote that, too; aesthetics happens to someone,

I suppose, or it doesn't, it doesn't happen
because a poet writes an essay and says,

"But, Aesthetics!"
This is my second Essay on Bad Writing.

*

In the first Essay on Bad Writing,
I was thinking about men

who say that women's writing is "bad"
because they are afraid to deal with what the women's writing says

and "badness" is so general and low-brow-high-brow
("I can tell this is a bad poem instinctively

so I don't have to demonstrate understanding it, but I'd do so
expertly were it worth my time, you can tell by how stylish my dismissal is")

that it lets them change the terms of the conversation
to one they are the masters of: their own taste.

And I was thinking about the many people who said
that a man's writing was "bad" because that's easier

than seeing its sexism as structural or meaningful
or evidence of something "bigger"

than an MFA's failure to have trained him in craft
or a BA's failure to have trained him to hide his sexism in mixed company

or whatever the fuck people care about when they say
something is poorly written, I'm not sure.

I was wrong, then, too—gender wasn't as important
as I sensed, and "performance" no longer strikes me as the question.

But here, no, I'm thinking about something else:
why anyone wants poetry to be mute and opinion-less.

Poetry makes arguments, I mean:
That's this book's argument,

I mean: I'm only writing poems
about something, for a little bit.

*

Lately, everything I write refutes something
I wrote earlier—even when the work remains unpublished, dying

peacefully. This makes my logic so circular, so directed at myself
that it's hard to know where to begin. A few years ago

I was trying to define "postconceptual" writing.
This term's been thrown around a lot, if less

often than its visual art counterpart—in *Anywhere
or Not at All*, Peter Osborne argues that

post-conceptuality "defines the state of visual art today." Felix Bernstein uses
"postconceptual" the most ridiculously; for him, it seems to offer

an umbrella term for the small group of writers at whom he doesn't want to
throw incomprehensible shade. For others, it's used to promise

a writer doesn't share Conceptual Writing's dumb, offensive
longing for some erasure of subjectivity: the "post" is a refusal.

Some are just trying to periodize, I guess.
I wrote that essay, but I don't want to put it here.

I wrote it just like a grad student: block quotes
from some philosophers, abstractions pitched as calls-to-action,

reflections on the "ineliminabilty of aesthetics,"
you get it—academia fucked up my style.

I start with it, though, because the arguments I tried to make
there led me to their opposites.

I was hung up on an incredibly limited sense
of what constituted a "literary purpose."

I started to call something "Fictional Poetry"—
i.e., poetry that uses the style, plot, characterization,

or forms of fiction. What's "fictional" is a quality of *aboutness*
that prevents overemphasis on form—and on the repetition

of forms that often characterize the appearance of schools—
and resists the belief that the shape a poem takes

is always the source of its politics / interestingness /
literariness / purpose. Instead, the books I want to write

about don't mind being about things: about love,
about childbirth, about borders, about sex, about gossip,

for example. Other writing is *about* things, too. But most
things that pass for poems

today are list poems without knowing it. This is one
reason for the term "Fictional"—no one is surprised that

fiction is about things.
But another is the sense of the *lie*:

the old utility of making-something-up to say something
"true." To whatever extent Elena Ferrante overlaps

with Elena in the Neapolitan novels,
the books' ability to unite

the "novel about the woman broken by love" with
the "novel in which an individual stands in

for the nation's political upheaval" with
the "novel about the way becoming a writer requires,

for most people, becoming an unforgivable class traitor"—
sets off a lot of fictional truths. We hold novelists accountable

for the worlds they build, we might ask them to
account for themselves, we're critical about what does

and does not get represented, and in how much detail, but we're also a lot better
at helping them maintain their contradictions.

One contradiction novels and their readers have been pretty good at
maintaining is that between conflicting voices.

It was the opposition between "monologic" and "dialogic"
writing that initially motivated me to think about fiction

in contemporary poetry. My interest in what might be *fictional*
comes from Mikhail Bakhtin, for whom the ability to balance

voices—the incorporation of what seems like someone's speech
other than the narrator's—is the defining characteristic

of the style of novelistic discourse: "social heteroglossia and
the variety of individual voices in it" are not exceptions

to a stylistic rule, but the mark of "authentic
novelistic prose." Bakhtin famously prioritizes this

quality of the novel in *opposition* to poetry, which (for him)
is essentially monologic. For Bakhtin,

individual elements of a novel's style
are "subordinated to the higher stylistic unity of the work as a whole,

a unity that cannot be identified with any single
of the unities subordinated to it" (262). If this was not true

for the poetry Bakhtin was reading (I'm not sure),
I think lots of poetries have conspired against monologue.

But more than lies, convos, content—you'll note that this idea
of "fiction" is incredibly broad and silly, and that it could

and does include movies, plays (anything where there's
A Fiction that comes together from smaller fictions)—

I mean, poems that tell stories.
I love a literal example. It spares criticism

the need to operate by way of analogies
or paranoid pattern-finding. One poem

in Monica McClure's *Tender Data* is literally titled "Bakhtin."
It's about narrative discourse. I'll admit that I was once put off

by the proliferation of academic language
in contemporary poetry, but now I feel like

poetry provides a better context for the lie of academic certainty
than does its unnatural habitat, the peer-reviewed article.

The anger here, that is, is real, and it's a sometimes academic
anger: the speaker's saying "fuck you" to her

academic readers in their own tongue. But it also says
go ahead, read this in terms of narrative discourse, tell me

what I'm saying, have fun quoting a line
almost certainly contradicted somewhere on the next page.

*

Yesterday, I went to a roundtable at Artists Space
with writers for Commune Editions—

Juliana, Jasper, Joshua, Jasmine, now that I name
them here, I'm reminded of Juliana's reading

where she changes the names of her friends
to the most popular baby names of 2015, to avoid

writing a "coterie" poem, she says;
I hope I'm not writing a coterie poem, but I'll risk it.

These are poets to whom you should not say,
"But, the Politics of Aesthetics!"

unless you want a response
ranging from a fuck-it eye roll to a mini-lesson

on the irrelevance of poetic invention to real struggle:
they, thank God, have not structured their press around hope

that some specific "new" form will be political,
even if the poet doesn't bother to fill it in

with anything remotely having to do with politics.
This hope plagues academic conferences on "the politics of poetry":

"the fragmentary image counters
the totalizing forces of capitalism," or

"the totalizing concept holds up a mirror
to capitalism" (capitalism is always being "shown"

its mirror images, in both senses,
and it gives no fucks, as far as I can tell)—

and they don't do "that other" thing either,
"political poetry will bring about the revolution,"

an even less likely syllabus
to incite the good riots.

*

(Here's how they framed poetry's relationship to politics in the event's
description: as the "'Riot Dog' of Athens . . . Some barking. Some letting

you know that the cops are at the door.")

*

So these writers haven't hung
their hopes for poetry on it doing more

than poetry does.
That's one way I'm down.

*

Jasmine was the only poet on the panel
who made what might be called an "aesthetic argument"

about her own work: she said that her poetry tells lies.
I wanted to ask about the function of telling a poetic lie,

but I worried, if I asked this question, it would seem like I was trying
to subtly disagree with the others' disinterest in identifying

a specific poetic function that might explain
why they are all always writing poems and being poets

which isn't what I wanted to ask. Not to challenge,
but to agree—like anyone who is a poet & accidentally

made it partly a job to write arguments about poetry, a job I wanted
mostly because it seemed more pleasant

on the average day than other jobs,
and it is, it's no lie, academia is fucking awful

but, if someone pays you well enough to do it, and if you can survive
its bigotry, its stupidity, its committees, it can be easier

than other work, like anyone in these circumstances
I really don't want to write a bunch of papers

defending poetry for being so charmingly pointless.
"Isn't it great," I could say, "that I spend my Sundays

doing the equivalent of writing love letters on a typewriter,
I'm very precious, don't you think, but don't worry,

this is a 'political' decision, I'm claiming my
droit à la paresse, as you know, sons know better

than fathers the pleasures of shirking work."
What sort of lie would this be?

Looking forward to the 2 Fish Combo + a side of hush
puppies I walked into Long John Silvers, where my mom
would also let me order a side of "Crumblies®," the pieces of fried
batter that fall off the fish in the grease and are then sprinkled
over the platters, which, off menu, they'd let you order
a whole tray of for 50 cents? 25? There is no official source
for nutritional information for Crumblies. I was jumping
up and down, waving my arms, shouting, "Mom,
she is so fat!" I repeated it. According to my mom,
I was practically dancing, pointing at a woman
eating the same combo. My mom struggled to stop me, but couldn't
find a way to explain, quickly, why "fat" was an insult. Given that
I had a pretty bad stutter, there's some chance the harassment
was extended by the difficulty of both "em" and "ef" sounds.
Instead, she explained the inverse, apologizing,
"From my daughter, this is a compliment." I was truly
happy and my mom so sorry. The woman smiled, said it was clear
I meant well. I got quiet, knowing, from my mom's face,
I had done something "wrong," in the worst way
—the kind where someone was hurt.
As we ate she explained it was fine
for me to feel excitement but it was not fine
to describe people's bodies to them.
I might have made the woman very sad, she said.

It seemed to me, then, that if you liked
someone, you would be delighted
when there was more of them. My happiest cats
got fat and we said "look how fat you have become, Butch,
we love you." Why else did we spend our lives

(the life a small child can imagine) in others' arms
as often as possible, our bodies curled around them?

Maggie Nelson throws her hands in the air and celebrates fatness
for a brief paragraph of *The Argonauts,* which I read on the train
from NYC to Montreal. It made me, at first, cry,
in the most normal way, deciding whether to want the kind of love
The Argonauts represents, one where two people become an actual unit,
everything they encounter forming a new private world;
dismissive accounts of Žižek support not just an "argument"
about the body, but also imply that Harry agreed
with the dismissals, or at least that they talked about
that section together, the way lovers do when they become editors.
I had interrupted my reading to write many drafts
of the same love letter, all unsendable—I wanted
so badly both to have such a you to address
and, I suppose, to find out how I felt.

The first attempts all stopped in starting:

> Dear dear,

> even there I stop. I have never sent you a letter, so "Dear X" is too inti-
> mate . . .

> Dear X . . . a letter's opening should be generic, should draw on some
> established familiarity, "to whom it may concern," "liebe," "Hi!" To
> address this to you, dear, is to begin with the end, yours, Diana: that's
> what's familiar to me, the sense that I don't want to be my own . . .

But I had a plan in mind: I was only reading *The Argonauts*
because he just had, and, following Shklovsky, I'm always looking
for something to replace love in the letter:

. . . I don't feel very calm because I just read *The Argonauts* in one sitting. I was excited when you told me you were reading it, and apprehensive, too, because you don't talk to me about books. As it is basically the only thing lovers have ever talked to me about, and as I am trying to be different from my past self, I have tried to not to assume that anyone wants me to talk about what I'm reading.

Anyway, Nelson recounts the experience of her and her mother's anxiety in the way I've always found most comforting for explaining it myself: a way of making sure you've dealt with everything bad that can happen in advance, as a kind of protection spell against it . . .

With each letter, it became clearer
1. that I knew I was not loved in return, 2. that I was "better
off," 3. that I wasn't prepared to gush about
The Argonauts, so 4. I came back
to the book and to my excitement
when Nelson turns, briefly, to fatness.

She talks about fatness purportedly to add
to the complicated set of ways one might feel
"at home" in one's body, in one's self. She says:

> It feels important to pause and pay homage to the fact that many of the many-gendered mothers of my heart—Schulyer, Ginsberg, Clifton, Sedgwick—are or were or have been corpulent beings.

But Nelson is quick to exclude herself
from this list, not just by fact of thinness, but by its
essentialness: "having a small body,
a slender body, has long been related to my sense
of self, even my sense of freedom." This is quite strange,
even if she's offering the fact by way of apology.

Is size a new element to add to the function
of an author's name; does "Nelson" carry
with it a thinness that "Sedgwick" doesn't?

I think Nelson brings up the corpulence of the many-
gendered mothers of her heart for many reasons—
most obviously, to attempt to cope with her own
mother, obsessed with thinness, but also
to acknowledge, albeit indirectly, that
"fatness" relates to her earlier rejection of the narrative
by which trans people are necessarily "trapped" by the body.
And, from another direction, also unstated, to note how
"body positivity"—language used to support love of fatness,
specifically—can become transphobic when it compels
people to love their bodies "as they are."
And to recognize a queerness in fatness,
if only in an indirect sense: that a queer space
or a queer sex would understand the body and its charms better:
when I first read Gertrude Stein's *Lifting Belly*,
for a class on "Modernist Poetry," the other students were shocked
not by the cunnilingus, but by the fatness of a belly
that needed to be moved out of the way to get to the clit.

It was the most erotic description of gay sex
I had experienced, and became somewhat constitutive
of my sense of it: I find myself disappointed
to learn many bellies don't need to be lifted,
even if some will permit you to
overeagerly lift the *mons pubis*.

By the fifth draft, the letters were addressed
to myself: it became clear that this was a diary. As such
it turned to my body, my frustrations with it,
and more earnestly to Nelson:

I don't understand whether to care about gaining weight. I was so excited when Nelson started talking about loving fat people, I wanted her to keep going, but then of course it turned out it was important to her to remain small. When I have been small I have been obsessed with looking at myself, literally pulling the loose sacks of skin where fat used to be up to photograph them, then to decide whether, if I encountered these sacks, I could still be attracted to someone, how in love I would need to be to see them as beautiful.

But Nelson limits the question
to one of motherhood. I wonder if she doesn't
account for the place of love of corpulence in this book
about bodies and love because she's thin, one, and
two, because "fat," among other categories
(like "woman" or "poor") can sometime be used as an excuse
for oppression. I fear here, for example, that my temptation to write
about my own body, to the extent that it has been or will become fat,
is another way to misguidedly cling
to whatever small piece of myself escapes power.

As with the fucking women. I have failed to finish
this essay many times, getting stuck on the question
of whether, like Nelson's paragraph, this is about my love
of others or of myself, and if the latter, whether
I am "thin." I am probably not, I suppose,
big enough to represent personal positivity
about it—nothing about my size has been interesting
except its changes: once, I found myself small
for a year or two, on account of anxiety-induced IBS.
I quit fainting and started shitting, then started fainting
from fear of shitting, and so I quit eating much from fear
of both fainting and shitting, and everywhere I went,
friends asked: "What is your secret? You look amazing."

In those moments, I thought, what a way to die, the body
deciding not to turn food into self, the self becoming
"beautiful" for there being less of her, to be prettier
every day until one day, so pretty, the great relief of collapse,
not the whiteout of a panic attack, but the permanent one,
where you never have to go to a party again. I saw my mom
get this kind of thin once, too: the years where she had cancer
removed from her face, around the time
she had a hysterectomy, still working the many jobs she worked
so that I, I suppose, could sit at home and grow softer, but
you will not be surprised this was not an easy time for her
to eat food. There were compliments: how did she lose
the weight, friends and family wanted to know? I remember
somewhere in these years going with her to shop for a new
swimsuit, feeling sad she took a smaller size than I did:
our souls are eaten away so early that we are jealous of our mom's
weight loss due to cancer in the swimsuit aisle.

Still, the hesitation here is that, for some reason,
I was very upset about Nelson's combining expression
of love of corpulence with insistence she herself
must be thin. It "hurt my feelings," as if
I were there in the book, too. So I wanted to write a poem,
a love letter to softness that would be different, I thought,
but could not write it for inability to describe myself.

Such that I started to feel, about the question of whether
the pounds I've gained back merit talking about,
the same way I feel about whether the women
I've slept with render me gay
enough to talk about queerness: this is what "bi-
sexuality" (you know it's not queer
when the vernacular for your sex life is like
"hey let's double down on this shit! I like both

there are only TWO things to like," god damn it) feels like,
a dull canceling out. It's a word
I've permitted myself only because it's abject ("adj.
(of a person or their behavior) completely without pride"):
to say "queer" is to claim something, to say "bi"
is to apologize. Soon there will be a word
that a girl known to also have boyfriends can say
of herself without pissing off lesbians, but
for now, "queer" pretends too much in common;
bi- pretends too many don't exist.
As with weight: "No, I don't want to
go to that store, they refuse to stock pants
I can get my thighs into, I can
still comfortably ride an airplane, please don't
'reassure' me that I am 'not fat' just take me
to the store that has pants for all of us, the queer
bar but for jeans." What I am trying to say is,
basically, that an average "bisexual" is a person
whose traits have not risen
to the dignity of a self and so require
other evidence—queerer, bigger desires.

A desire, for example, for a better interlocutor
for my body—someone eager to pick up
not just my belly, but the pieces, not just
of myself, but of the things I am reading, and
of the memories of family grafted
onto them: for example, to write to someone
who would want to hear how, in trying to finish
this poem, I read a 2014 "scientific" study that concluded
that, because "compared with heterosexual women
. . . lesbians and bisexuals had increased likelihood
of being overweight at age 18 years and maintaining
overweight status during adulthood," they had found

"a need for interventions for sexual minority
women" (the study found that queerness
was *protective* against obesity for men). Truly:
the scientists want to "intervene" with teenage
women who like women to warn them
that they are more likely to become fat. When I
was seventeen, I went to a gynecologist
for a recurring yeast infection that turned out
(after six months of incredible sexual pain)
to have been repeatedly transmitted by the then-
boyfriend, and the doctor noted I had checked "bisexual"
on the form. "I have to warn you," he offered,
"that you're at much greater risk of contracting HIV."
"That is not true," I laughed. He repeated: "I'm not
homophobic—this is me trying to better treat gay
patients," in Indiana, he specified, where many doctors
still pretended gay people didn't exist. "I understand,"
I said, "But I listed the number of sexual partners
and their genders. I'm not sure how my unrequited love
for other women is likely to lead to infection."
He also, I might note, recommended
I lose about 20 pounds:
"You should be careful, is all I'm saying."

I'll watch or read hours of garbage if it seems like there's a good kiss coming up.

This is how I returned to binge watching television, having given it up about as many times as I've quit smoking (another good way to pass pre-kiss time). While I once spited the sometimes 20-hours of screen-time waiting for the answer to "will they?" to become a sloppy "yes," I finally learned the pleasure in seeing it coming, and in doing the math ("we're only halfway through a season, and that kiss would be in a finale, be patient"), in finding out just how much boring plot (*"Does* she get into *that* Northeast Ivy League school, or the other?! How *will* this 'poor' family make it in their fancy Connecticut suburb, in Dumbo, in LA?") I'll put up with in anticipation of seeing two fictional people make out.

My possible wait time is longest where a woman's desire is primarily at stake. This is how I watched so many seasons of *The Good Wife*: waiting for a moment where Will would kiss Alicia from behind, allowing the camera to catch both of their faces in not-quite-overlapping profile, her clavicles front-and-center, his eyes joining the camera's on her neck, which strains while she struggles to kiss him without rotating her torso (this is not the first kiss, where he holds her face in his hands, as if afraid she will pull back—it's some unspecified later kiss, but it will do).

This "waiting" cannot be spoiled; it's not that kind of suspense. The kiss I'm waiting for is not one I plan to be surprised by, and in fact, it's all the better if I'm rewatching the show, rereading the book, or have had the plot told by a friend. Then, what I'm watching is just narrative structure, since I generally remember the loose outlines of what happens but forget what the camera/narrator/syntax will do to get me there.

Rereading shifts suspense's genre: on first take, some works' suspense remains structured by the question "What is going to happen?" Second takes rely on the more bewildering "How am I going to feel as it happens, compared to how I felt a few years go?" or "How did it happen, again?" or "*Oh*, why didn't I notice this before?" Some books let you know from the beginning that someone will certainly be married, fucked, or killed before the book's back matter, yes, but rereading lets us know equally that subterranean gnomes are inevitably on their way to work in the mines, or that a woman will crack open her skull as narrative punishment for taking the protagonist's man.

This is not about the pleasure of rereading, though, about which much has been written (especially by men who believe it protects them from novelty, against which it is a terrible shield): all teachers know you ought to, all students know it's a chore, and all children know no other reading at all. The end.

*

When I first started writing this essay, it was a failed reading of the sex scenes in George R. R. Martin's *A Song of Ice and Fire* series, mapped onto D.A. Miller's reading of Jane Austen, in terms of the experience of reading each as a young girl, then rereading them as a (still young, but a decade or two older) woman. The second version hinged on the observation that women never penetrate men in Martin's series, reading this as a stand-in for a larger inability of women to actually gain control, even in a narrative founded on the fantasy of an eventual matriarchy. The third version, an attempt at a pitch for a journal of contemporary erotics, focused instead on the kind of watcher-of-porn who simply re-watches 1-minute trailers until "finished." In each version, I wrote:

> Rereading is, of course, the sexiest of readings. Books are no place for that most abhorrent kink, the love of the first time.

As I sit down to write this version, I see that I unconsciously plagiarized this comparison from Roland Barthe's *S/Z*, which I haven't read since college. I thought, "isn't it weird to get this far into an essay on rereading without quoting even the most famous theorists of reading?" "Yes, it is," I agreed with myself, so I put "rereading" and "Barthes" into the search bar, and found the passage in *S/Z* where he laments the way the second reading is

> unjustly condemned by the commercial imperatives of our society which compels us to squander the book, to discard it as though it were deflowered, in order to buy a new one—this retrospective reading bestows upon Sarrasine's kiss a precious enormity.

Barthes is also reading a kiss, in this passage, one whose meaning changes when you reread "Sarassine" with the knowledge that the titular character has misjudged the gender of the person he kisses. When irony is not dramatic, but at the reader's expense, it takes a second reading to feel at all clever.

The fourth time I sat down to write this essay, I was rewatching *Buffy the Vampire Slayer.* I wasn't just waiting for a kiss; I was waiting for season six, when Buffy and Spike hate-fuck as the building collapses around them. Somehow, I was unable to skip to that episode, or even to that season: I was watching from the beginning to remember what, in the fictional structure of her romantic life, leads her to that moment (the repetition of desire for the vampire, of course, along with a more complicated sense of what it means to "have a soul" or "be a demon"—rewatching *Buffy*, the early scenes where Angel treats her mercilessly—because, we believe on first watch, he can't show love without a soul—become much darker; now that we know that Spike found a way to love her even without one, we see Angel for what he is: an abusive boyfriend hiding behind the excuse of an illness).

You might roll your eyes at me and at Barthes (it's so nice to put oneself in good resented company) and say that it's more pleasurable to *find out* what happens than to watch it play out again. It's not about a deflowering, you'd argue, but about falling in love for the first time.

But this is bullshit. You're not "discovering" anything; the show already exists; everyone else already watched it, or is watching it at once; there's no pleasure to be had in not knowing; the only pleasure is understanding. We watch repetitive trash on TV because we like to understand; we reread our favorite books because we feel we know them; we call up old friends with whom we have little in common because we'd like to be able to refer to stories from our shared pasts: "Do you remember when, in middle school, we co-wrote two seasons of a TV show called *Keeping in Touch*, in which we imagined all reuniting in twenty years and checking the facts of our depressing marriages and more-interesting careers against our memories of sitting in that dining hall?" "Remember when I chained a boy to a tree during my first kiss, because I misread (or read too soon) his interest in dog-earing all the sexy bits of Stephen King novels, but it turned out teenage boys don't yet know they want to be chained to trees?" We want to tell a story to someone who cuts us off to say, "I've heard this before, Diana."

I don't mean to literally suggest that nothing happens the first time you read a thing. Obviously, I like learning shit, which you have to do a first time in order to keep doing, the same attitude with which I approached "loss of virginity." But lets think about that "love of the first time" Barthes thinks gets in the way of loving rereading: it's the false attachment to this idea that makes, for example, penetrative sex necessary to end "virginity" for most people in the U.S., even though, for the happiest narratives of becoming-a-person-who-has-sex, there's lots of other sex that comes before and after that. And for a teenager with a vagina having sex with people with dicks, the thing that is "lost" by "finally" having vaginal sex is often not virginity, but the opportunity to do something other than be boringly penetrated by your lover for the rest of your relationship.

I'm pretending I don't understand the pleasure of reading something for the first time, because this lie helps me get to a point:

*

Grad school discourages you (here, you=me) from finding pleasure in rereading. In this context, it becomes a job requirement. You reread the texts you're writing about because you must do so to "master" them for the sake of the argument; you're looking for something other critics have missed, for a mistake in your own, already-written reading, for quotes that support the argument you've already intended to make. But for the most part you don't even read whole books anymore. There are individual chapters in this-or-that monograph that you refer to without having read the others (if you're careful, you skim the index for any key terms in other sections that might relate to your argument); there are essays by "important theorists" that might give your argument the dignity of an apparent method. For the books that don't relate to your scholarship at all, it becomes increasingly less likely you're reading them once, let alone twice. You keep either mental or physical lists of books you ought to have read, and when you decide, for example, you'd like to revisit that novel you read the summer after college that gave you the idea for the project you proposed when you applied to grad school (which, with any luck, you've moved beyond), you feel guilty at the thought of reading a book again at the expense of another, one that would enable you to say "yes" at a post-conference dinner where another academic asks, "Have you read X?"

This is one reason I'm writing a book of essays structured around repudiations of prior opinions: rereading myself, I reject what I've read before, write again, reread, write again, reread, eventually let an editor become the rereader, if I'm lucky to have the option of ceding that authority, and then reread again, once things can't be changed, and come to accept the text as it changes anyway, because of "time."

Barthes goes so far as to suggest this worst-case scenario—rereading for mastery—doesn't even exist:

> Thus it would be wrong to say that if we undertake to reread the text we do so for some intellectual advantage (to understand better, to analyze on good grounds): it is actually and invariably for a ludic advantage.

Another (less direct) translation makes more direct the relationship to kissing: "it is in fact and always for an increase in pleasure," quoted in Robert

Scholes' *Structuralism in Literature*, not quite what you might get from "c'est en fait et toujours pour un profit ludique," but that depends on how you play. Either way, he argues that there's never a real longing for mastery in the reencounter, only the playfulness of what changes with familiarity.

What changed in the initial rereadings that led me to write this essay, though, was not necessarily playful. Rereading both Austen and Martin required a rejection of an adolescent version of myself to which I had held on as long as I needed to: a girl who saw herself, despite all evidence to the contrary, somehow immune to the conditions of gender. The librarian who insisted I read *Pride and Prejudice* didn't understand that I already *knew* I wasn't interested in Austen, as I certainly wasn't interested in marriage, wealth, tradition, family, or heterosexuality. When I finally fell in love with Austen, 15 years later, I learned the librarian might have been appealing to my interest in the sentence.

But there was nothing so painful in the loss of resistance to Austen on second read. It's true, I didn't know, when I was a kid, that it was interesting in itself to read a book by a woman, as it had never been brought to my attention that the books assigned to me were written by men. Realizing, at the start of a doctoral program, that professors saw themselves as going above-and-beyond if they even considered assigning books by women wasn't the most ludic experience.

But I was *pleased* to find so much of myself in the way I had first tried to read her, in the same way that, on rereading Martin, I was pleased to find so much of a self I had left behind in high school: one who would take a book for feminist because 1. It didn't assume women wouldn't read it, just because it was violent genre-fiction, and 2. It passed the Bechdel test.

*

Here, I'm trying to help the first time seem like the second.

Imagine the essay began one of the following ways:

*

No one gets pegged in George R. R. Martin's *A Song of Ice and Fire.*

*

Lionel Trilling dies without answering the titular question to his essay, "Why Do We Read Jane Austen?" But one answer is simple: because we happen to have already read Jane Austen earlier, and we want to remember how we felt.

*

Most of the middle-aged men I sexted with in text-based RPGs as a child, I found out, thought it was clear that I was *also* a middle-aged man.

*

In the opening essay to D. A. Miler's *Jane Austen, or the Secret of Style*, he writes to a shared "we" who all seem to be men who, though now queer, read Jane Austen in their youth without realizing it would mark them as such. More specifically, he reads Austen's style, on first encounter, as hinging on the narrator's impersonality, signed by style's very defense of impersonality, only to realize that, to everyone else, whether "we" knew it or not, this style goes by the name of Woman.

When I read George R.R. Martin in high school, I thought it guaranteed I *wouldn't* be read as a girl. Reading genre fiction, I thought, instead, that I was like Arya Stark; in fact, my first AOL screenname was Arya Bombadil, joining the best Stark with Tolkien's singing secondary character (I guess I wanted to be, at once, a straight-girl-dressed-as-a-dyke-who-learns-to-be-a-great-murderer and a gay-man-who-took-his-beard-by-force-and-who-may-be-the-oldest-creature-in-existence-but-who-hides-that-by-singing-in-rhyme?).

When I started reading *A Song of Ice and Fire*, I had the same reaction to the female characters in *A Game of Thrones* most men did: I thought Arya was awesome, and that Sansa was stupid and deserved whatever she had coming. It was only as Martin added on punishment after punishment—specifically, when Sansa tries to hide the fact that she's gotten her period to avoid being raped—that I realized the set up. Within the realm of the narrative, Sansa's not being "punished" per se; she's just experiencing the world as women do. But within the world of the books' *fans*, Sansa's plight in King's Landing is comeuppance for her stupid femininity. I think that Martin tries to scaffold the slow revealing of her torture in order to reverse this course, in a familiar narrative move: he loves to rehabilitate a "complicated" character that seemed earlier maligned (facilitated by his use of chapters limited to the POV of individual characters). With Sansa, though, this works much less well to change fan's reactions than it does to even Jaime—being effectively socialized as a woman is less forgivable than, say, attempting to murder that woman's little brother.

But hating this kind of femininity is often how you gain entrance, as a young girl, to the respect of men, especially to "nerd" men. If you show up at the arcade, the D&D game, whatever, you show that you're laid back enough to not mind the rape scenes, you laugh when they talk about the violent porn they watch (that you watch, too), you agree that the dumb pretty girls who reject these boys are vapid monsters. This is true especially if, in the way middle schools are often structured, these girls seem like *your* tormentors more than theirs, especially if you still have hope they'll hear in this news of their own vapidity reason to kiss you instead. You can wait all summer.

*

Here's a related story about rereading: in middle school, I spent a great deal of time in MUDs (Multi-User Dungeons), RPGs where the world was navigated entirely by text. For example, you type "N" to move north; text appears telling you there's a squirrel on your square; you can type a command to do something to the squirrel, like, "Look at squirrel," which will generally produce a description of the squirrel, etc.—you proceed through a map with language.

The squirrel is a planned element of the fictional world, so it has a description attached to it. But when you interact with other users directly, you have to produce the description yourself. Which means that, if you were me, you might say (or "whisper") "13yo/F/Indiana" if asked, and then, if the tall 42 year old wizard from Ohio asked you to, start attempting to describe the oral sex you were pretending to perform.

I really wish I had access to these transcripts now; I would love to know what baby-Diana thought to type when she tried to write sex scenes to strange old men as an elf. But there's one part I do remember: after the "sex" was over, and we moved on to talking about ourselves in other ways, many men would surprise me by revealing their *first read* of our initial encounter.

"So, where are you really from? Tell me about yourself," they'd insist. It would take me some time, given my interest in full sentences, to convince them that I was actually in the 8th grade, actually a woman (an adult woman was already a pretty unlikely person to wind up on these sites). Some men then *panicked*, apologized; one finally explained that he assumed my age/sex combo was as much a fantasy as the rest—I was Moephenia Deborone, 6', blue-skinned, magical. Why not also be a teenager?

Most of the middle-aged men I had text-based sex with in these MUDs as a child, I found out, thought it was clear that I was also a middle-aged man, one choosing a clearly-implausible role for the sake of fantasy.

This was before there were widely-circulated news stories warning about the dangers of online predation, before there were sting operations as easy-to-watch TV. When forced to reread our encounter with the understanding of my age and gender, they were horrified; these men certainly preferred the way they read the first time.

*

I shared their horror, given how hard I thought I was working, at this point, not to be a 13-year-old girl. This longing was so real that it involved amnesia for much of my childhood: I started insisting I had never been "feminine," had never liked pink, had never liked dresses, until one day my brother overheard me and reminded me that I had been exaggeratedly invested in all such things until puberty.

If nerd shit was my way out of being-a-girl, it was also my way back in: every time a girl in Martin attempts to gain power (or succeeds, even), or attempts to transcend the limits of gender, someone shows up and reminds her what she is, generally at knife-point or dick-point. As this happened increasingly throughout the books, it happened to me reading them as well; like Miller, I realized that my reading was revealing the name Woman in me just where I thought I had escaped it.

*

If one thing unites the way I read at 13 and the way I read at 30, it's the willingness to admit that I'm anticipating whatever kiss, love letter, or sex act the book has set me up to look forward to. The same girl who dog-eared the demon-assault scenes in Anne Rice now begs her roommate permission to read aloud the moment in *Chelsea Girls* where Myles says, in a description of fucking a john, "I had no sympathy for his possible disappointment."

For the ages in between, I had worked hard to ward off this kind of reading, where I was mainly engaged with my own satisfaction of an anticipation— perhaps the most base version of the poetics of "absorption" so many of the poets I grew up reading rejected—for the sake of something more intellectual, more engaged with form, more about having authority over the text.

I guess it took getting a PhD to find reading books because I like them non-embarrassing.

Let's watch Bran (age seven) watch Jaime and Cersei have sex, right before Jaime pushes Bran out of the window:

> Inside the room, a man and a woman were wrestling. They were both naked. Bran could not tell who they were. The man's back was to him, and his body screened the woman from view as he pushed her up against a wall.
>
> There were soft, wet sounds. Bran realized they were kissing. He watched, wide-eyed and frightened, his breath tight in his throat. The man had a hand down between her legs, and he must have been hurting her there, because the woman started to moan, low in her throat. "Stop it," she said, "stop it, stop it. Oh, please . . ." But her voice was low and weak, and she did not push him away. Her hands buried themselves in his hair, his tangled golden hair, and pulled his face down to her breast.

Martin wants the POV to defamiliarize the violence of sex, to imagine what reading sex for the first time might look like. But Bran's point-of-view gets accidentally mingled with the genre's. "Tangled golden hair" makes it seem like Bran wants Jaime, whereas the titillation is supposed to rest with the reader.

In these chapters, though, the limited focalization is primarily for the sake of making things less clear; it doesn't matter whether ambiguity is consistent with the limitation of the viewer.

When Bran "could not tell who they were," it literally suggests that he just doesn't recognize Jaime and Cersei. But on second read, it also implies he can't tell them apart, as Cersei says her father couldn't when they were little. It's not just Cersei and Jaime the books want to keep confusing, though; there's a broader fantasy that, even in penetrative sex, roles could get mixed up:

as the sun was coming up, she used her mouth to make him hard again, as Doreah had taught her long ago, then rode him so wildly **that his wound began to bleed again**, and for one sweet heartbeat **she could not tell whether he was inside of her, or her inside of him.**

Sure, the women can't take power without suffering a level of misogyny that somehow makes itself palpable even in addition to the world's baseline level of torture, but Daenerys can fuck her husband so enthusiastically he gets his period. There's a similar scene where Asha Greyjoy (Yara on the show), sleeps with Qarl the Maid, whom she introduces to peaches:

Asha draped the furs across her bare shoulders and mounted him, **drawing him so deep inside her that she could not tell who had the cock and who the cunt.** This time the two of them reached their peak together. (368)

Much has been written/yelled/bemoaned about the sex—especially violent sex and rape—in *Game of Thrones*. It was weird for me when all my friends started watching the show, given that, at some point, I had started pretending not to like Martin.

But on second read, this what I take from the books: that the het sex scenes betray his fantasy for a narrative not founded in women's torture, for the ease of a "role reversal" on a broader geographic and literary scale.

These sex scenes are about Martin not wanting the books to be for men, even as I wanted, on first read, the fact that they were for men to mean they were also for *me*, a girl, even as TV ensured the narrative be adapted for men's eyes, etc.: if you read the book again, you'll find not only a different book, one (one hopes) better in having been despoiled, but also a different reader's desire.

GOD WAS RIGHT.

We were wrong.

"Cats are good"

God is right when He suggests that "cats are good," and that He is "well-pleased" with cats.

He is right to kiss them, and to pet their orange, short fur, made softer by supplements, and their long, grey fur, which makes them look old when they are young, and their tortoiseshell fur, with missing patches from rashes produced by chewing at fleabites, and the space of fur between their over-long ears, and the part under their chin that they like the most, and to kiss each of the beds of their toes in succession,
all while He pets another cat, at the same time, who has an additional toe, while that cat plays with a dead mouse, etc.

Cats are good,
He reminds us, every time we come across a cat. Take, for example, Easy, who was missing a leg and all teeth but one.

God was right to make me watch her die:

He wanted me to experience the stupidity of my sentimental attachment to pets in the midst of global catastrophe,
the smallness of the sorts of things we are given to care for so that we can remember not to care for those things that, if we did, would require a complete overall of the structure of life, the murder of most men alongside the same men's defense of murder as a necessary means of establishing a better world, the replacement of the bad world with a world somehow less doomed to perpetual badness;
He wanted me to become the immortal protagonist of de Beauvoir's *All*

Men are Mortal, the title of which suggests that said protagonist must have been misgendered:

women live forever, in order to see that there is no point in love, or in cats.

God made up for Easy's missing leg and teeth by growing a tumor on her mammary gland, one with a nipple on the end that gave the impression she was growing one small tit, and by a terrible, high-pitched yowl, itself also growing, along with her kidney disease, her heart murmur, her lung cancer, her bloody sneezes, and her habit of hogging the bed and peeing where she shouldn't.

This is her legacy, as the diseases and the leglessness continue despite her recent death, and will forever, not like a famous novel, but like something worse:
like God, and his stupid lessons.

We're told we can recognize God by the fact that cats never walk on Him.

Easy recently saved my life.

She was right to save my life.

Burroughs is right when he dreams of a cat for whom he does not know how to care.

Cats are sometimes dream cats, that is to say, and it is difficult to know with accuracy

1. whether a cat in question is dreamt,
2. whether one is dreaming,
3. whether one has anything to offer a cat, or
4. anyone for that matter, as

5. we are all alone, even or especially in life, where we are most useless, but this is ok because, like cats, perhaps we
6. do "not offer services.

The cat offers itself." In which case, the question of what we have to offer the dream cat is the question of whether we have ourselves to offer,
which is a question cats cannot answer but which, to their credit, they know better than to ask.

A dream cat can offer itself.

God would be right if he let me have the dreams I'd like to have:

One where I'm a dog, and where I experience life the way dogs do, including smells and family and disease and being lonely, only to realize that growing up is hard for dogs, only to wake up with no ability to process the dream, because dog-sadness can't be translated to mine.

When Easy saved my life, she was a dream cat; Easy was also a non-dream cat, but this did not prevent her from being dreamed, or from saving.

One where I quit smoking, so that I don't have to do so in real life.

Montaigne is right when he wonders whether his cat plays with him, rather than he with it. When Easy saved my life it was non-metaphorical and dreamt, and also involved no services: I realized I could only escape attack by touching the cat, who would sacrifice some aspect of herself in the touching to save me; she sacrificed her two remaining teeth (for in the dream, Easy was a two-toothed cat, and had somewhat more "self" to offer).

When the man fell from the top of the tree and snapped his neck, Easy was also there, useless in breaking his fall, but a big help nonetheless.

We are right to entertain each other these ways.

Debbie is right when she acknowledges her failure to hug enough cats.

It is right to hug all of them, whereas I would estimate she—that is, I—has/ve hugged no more than 300 cats, including Merlin, whose birth preceded mine, Hobbes, whose birth preceded the hug, but followed my birth, which is true for all other cats in this list, to my knowledge, Butch, who slept in her food-dish, Sprite, who drank Sprite, Spice, who died, as did most other cats in this list, to my knowledge, Houdini, who I last hugged while crying while another family took him away, Foster Cat, who was denied a name to prevent the attachment demonstrated in the final hug of Houdini, Cassandra and Thomas, whom my dad gave back to the pound, Oliver, who bit my butt goodnight at approximately 10PM for many years, Bob, who lived with me, as did every cat in this list so far, to my knowledge, Easy, who saved my life, Davis, who wandered my school building, Émile/Monster, in whom Oliver's desire to bite was reincarnated to a much greater degree, countless cats in shelters, who had names I do not know, or had multiple names, or none, and a number of friends' cats: Brisby, Billy, Bunch, Ceefur, Dorothy, Feller, Hamlet, Millie, Pony, Tess, etc.

The virgin Mary, who prays for us sinners but does not pray for cats (who neither want for nor want God's approval) identifies four reasons that cats are good:

1. their real physical attributes,
2. their real non-physical attributes,
3. their imaginary physical attributes, and
4. their imaginary non-physical attributes.

Mary is right.

Cats are 1. soft, furry, cute, warm 2. perfect, smart, comforting, 3. immortal, and 4. magical and dreamt.

Let me give some examples.
Yesterday, a cat stood on my shoulders and kissed my head.

In this, the cat took advantage of a few of its real physical and non-physical attributes: I felt an immediate happiness all through my body, as if the cat's kiss had moved straight down to my toes, and this was made possible by how soft its face was, and how it rubbed cat-scent all over my glasses while it kissed me. Its excellent balance also enabled it to stand on my shoulders with little trouble, which also made it seem exceptional, since my own 3-legged Easy lacked such grace. In doing so, she also took advantage of her imaginary physical and non-physical attributes: as in my imagination of her specialness (physical), even though she was entirely cat-like; in her seeming to have missed me, which is unlikely but reassuring (non-physical), and in the fact that her kiss intervened in my next 24 hours, medicinally, so that anything bad that happened was forced to encounter the kiss of the cat as counter-example.

The same happens with movies, which are also good.

One in which I never have to live again, or to die, and neither does anyone else I know.

"So are dogs"

But people are wrong, however, when they fail to give up the false opposition that supports most defenses of cats inaccurately

—not that the desire to defend cats is inaccurate, but the method of defending, or the defense itself—

by contrasting them with dogs.

Not that dogs and cats are identical: let's not be silly.

It is almost always simple enough to tell them apart:

one loves you or doesn't, more or less; they have differently shaped noses; dogs are mortal and cats aren't; dogs are often bigger.

But they also share many things: both may love you, in fact; both may die, after their own fashion; both will inevitably get cancer; both enter your dreams.

It is not that one is a cool alien licking its paw in pristine indifference, while the other eats its own shit and awaits its death.

Although that, too, is true, it does not explain how dogs are worse: it's right to eat shit and wait to die.

In this, the best argumentative approach to the cat/dog relationship appears in the annual calendars on sale at any respectable mall, which offers one picture of a dog-cat pair for each month of the year. If you yourself struggle to understand that dogs, like cats, are good, the best remedy for this is to gather with friends on the 28th, 29th, 30th, or 31st—whichever is the last day of the given month—and guess what the dog and cat for the following month will look like.

Regardless of whether you guess accurately, your consideration of cat/dog shapes provides a meditative function that can be curative for your relationship to both animals and to yourself.

After you have performed this ritual for a year, you will be prepared to internalize it and perform it consistently, unconsciously, and to also think similarly about the people around you, imagining what form they will take the following month, and whether they will, so to speak, be cuddling their friends in baskets, in laundry-piles, in grass, or in hell.

"Read," God said

It is stupid to imagine that cats, or really anything, are perfect.

Sure, you are, and I am especially, occasionally stupid,

and it is right to be this kind of stupid when a cat is standing on your shoulders.

But when given the opportunity to reflect more calmly, in the absence of cats, it should be clear that there are ways cats could improve.

The most important way cats are imperfect is that they are completely incapable of learning to read.

A cat has never spent all day reading a novel, and so cannot recommend a good one, let alone loan one to you.

When I asked Easy, in fact, she had no response at all.

This a flaw in any companion, and would be especially unacceptable in a boyfriend.

For this and other reasons, cats make terrible boyfriends.

You cannot have sex with them, or talk to them about books, and they cannot say "I love you" in any human language.

A proposal: reading is better than cats.

If I had to choose between never being able to read again and never being able to hug a cat again, I would give up the cats.

Do not ask me to choose between destroying all existing books and all existing cats, though.

I would destroy the former.

On the other hand, it is right to fill the library with books rather than cats, not only because it is typical of libraries, but also because, if every possible combination of whatever makes a cat individual were iterated in a bunch of hexagonal rooms, the results would be similar to those of the books—the cats would go unread, which is to say, unloved, unfed, unpet—but the consequences would be more ghastly, millions of cat corpses packed tightly against each other in the stacks.

"But it is wrong"

we are told, to think "too much." "Don't think about it too much." "Just calm down and try to accept."

Some of you might ask:

Why does God tempt us to think about it too much if he doesn't want us to?

Because he wants us to suffer.

"Personally I"

hope to never wake up again, God said, and in saying, woke up, as if the words were a surprising sort of spell, and made coffee.

God was right to make coffee despite His suicidal ideation.

"Dancing is good"

When Herodias' daughter danced for Herod and demanded the head of John the Baptist on a platter, she was right.

One is always right to dance, whether or not it results in someone's death.

Of course dancing is dangerous: if you had not danced, you would not have gone home with so and so, you would have gotten up early the next morning and had a better work day, you would not have made a fool of yourself, or drunk so much, or ruined your best dress

(or so pleased a man that he granted you wishes, at the exact time when you happened to have wished for murder).

Since it is good to dance, it remains good to have danced.

But how do we know it is good?

Does dancing make you smarter, or is it good for children?

Does it encourage self-discipline?

Does it calm you down, or cast your fears away?

Does it bring good weather, or unite people in ritual behavior conducive to other good things?

Does it help you lose weight, or center yourself, or fall in love?

God would never ask these questions.

Cats would never ask these questions.

"Use the internet if you want to"

or don't, God suggests;

it's full of awful people and will ruin your life, but if you have access to it, you will come off as pretentious if you don't.

"I am sorry for this," God asks me to tell you.

But one day soon, the internet will be destroyed.

We will return to the arms of our dead cats, decomposing in our finite but huge libraries.

ACKNOWLEDGMENTS

"Attempt to Be Adequate to the Experience of Loving an Animal" appeared in *BOMB Magazine*, "Essay on Bad Writing" in *Prelude*, "2nd Essay on Bad Writing" in *Convolution*, "Persuasive Essay for Sex Ed" in *The Fanzine*, "Five-Paragraph Essay on Third Heartbreak" in *Tender*, "God Was Right" in *Arava Review*, and "Expository Writing on Some Kisses" in *Triangle House Review* and on the B.A.D. mixtape #1 for SALTS. Parts of this manuscript were written during the BHQFU Residency and the Blackacre Writing Residency.